THE ESSAYS OF BLUPETE:

LAW & POLITICS

Peter Landry

www.blupete.com

To "Lisa."

Report Errors: errata@blupete.com

Note for Librarians: A cataloguing record for this book is available from Library and Archives Canada at www.collectionscanada.ca/amicus/index-e.html
ISBN 1-4251-1437-7

PUBLISHING™
Offices in Canada, USA, Ireland and UK

Book sales for North America and international:
Trafford Publishing, 6E–2333 Government St.,
Victoria, BC V8T 4P4 CANADA
phone 250 383 6864 (toll-free 1 888 232 4444)
fax 250 383 6804; email to orders@trafford.com
Book sales in Europe:
Trafford Publishing (UK) Limited, 9 Park End Street, 2nd Floor
Oxford, UK OX1 1HH UNITED KINGDOM
phone +44 (0)1865 722 113 (local rate 0845 230 9601)
facsimile +44 (0)1865 722 868; info.uk@trafford.com
Order online at:
trafford.com/06-3196

10 9 8 7 6 5 4 3 2

Table Of Contents:

"On Liberty."

Liberty of each, limited by the like
liberties of all, is the rule in conformity
with which society must be organized.
— Herbert Spencer.

In 1941, F. D. Roosevelt said something that was to spur on the American soldier in his fighting efforts. Roosevelt held out that they would receive the complete support of those at home, and upon their return to America, better times were in store for all.

In the future days we look forward to a world founded upon four essential human freedoms. The first is freedom of speech and expression. The second is freedom of every person to worship God in his own way. The third is freedom from want. The fourth is freedom from fear.[1]

Highflown notions to which Aldous Huxley, in 1950, responded:

To talk about the Rights of Man and the Four Freedoms in connection with India is merely a cruel joke.

These notions, as gushed from Roosevelt's mouth, set the stage in what was to be, like so many freedom stealing programs of government, temporary, measures to ease ex-soldiers back with sympathy into an economic way of life supported on "the newly-painted pillars of the four freedoms." (Church.) Roosevelt made a mess of the classic notion of freedom; and so has most every other western politician who has followed in Roosevelt's steps, since. For, the notion of freedom as held by the ancient Greeks, as will be readily seen, was not so much "freedom from want"; but rather, "freedom from men."

What is Freedom?

One might go beyond the realm of reality and visualize or imagine that freedom is a state whereby one is free from the control of fate or of necessity. For the less fanciful: freedom might be conceived as an exemption or release from slavery or imprisonment. But freedom is more than that: it is personal: it is an exemption or release from "arbitrary, despotic, or autocratic control," as the *OED* has put it. It is "the power of self-determination attributed to the will": it is independence: it is the state of being able to act without hindrance or restraint: it is liberty of action.

Oliver Wendell Holmes described it as the "right of strict social discrimination of all things and persons, [and it] is one of the most precious privileges." And, John Locke: "... in our being able to act, or not to act, according as we shall choose, or will." And, Lord Acton: "By liberty I mean assurance that every man shall be protected in doing what he believes to be his duty against the influence of authority and majorities, custom and opinion."

It is not likely that anyone of us has had a cup of it this morning; nor, is it likely, that anyone of us has a special stash of it under a floor board. Freedom is not a physical thing, it's not to be directly sensed. It's a concept: it's a mental construct; it's a — Well, it's a — a state of affairs — that's what freedom is. Should you find yourself, in a damp dungeon with only two exits — the one covered with bars and which looks out over a moat many feet down, and the other covered by a great door bolted from the outside (and maybe, just for good measure, a great brute of a man with a machine gun stationed just outside) — you will quickly conclude that you are beset by a sad state of affairs. Equally as well, but likely even considerably more so, you would have the same reaction if somebody had a gun pointed at your head — in which event, you have arrived at a very sad state of affairs, indeed. In these two illustrations one might say that there exists a state of freedom (a state which cannot be described in absolute terms), which, practically speaking, is non-existent. There does not exist for a human, nor will it ever happen, unless you believe in heaven, that a perfect state of affairs will come about for any of us. Freedom normally comes to each of us but it can only exist in degrees; it is essential, I argue, to life itself; and it is most certainly expungable, especially if your adversary comes equipped with prisons and guns.

I would like to make it as plain as possible, that while freedom is not a measurable physical thing (and thus, it cannot be measured by any objective standard), it does exist for all humans up to the very point of his or her death, and does so by degrees. One might be restricted a little and get on with life quite well; indeed, a little general restriction, paradoxically, is necessary so that the most amount of freedom can be had by all (and there you have the *raison d'etre* for government). There is a point, however, at which a limitation of freedom will effect our well-being, and if freedom be taken away, then the person effected will, in time, die. Freedom for this reason is, as I will further elaborate, fundamental to life, to one's existence. It can be in a way likened to the air we breath, there is normally no joy in the act or in the experience, but its absence will bring about misery and death. To the extent we have freedom we have the ability to proceed in life to make the necessary decisions in life which suit our individual purposes.

Freedom is the general state of affairs in which we exist; it allows a person to take action, which, whether calculated or not,[2] is personally tailored and designed to suit the goals and objectives which the individual actor has set for himself, or herself. The ultimate goal (entirely predictable) for all sane and healthy individuals (the great mass of us) is to advance, on the medium term, the interests of themselves and/or the members of their particular family.

The Nature of Freedom:

> The root of all well-ordered social action is a sentiment of justice, which at once insists on personal freedom and is solicitous for the like freedom of others; and there at present exists but a very inadequate amount of this sentiment.   — Herbert Spencer.

It is necessary that a person grasp the meaning of freedom: it is no easy task. If a person is to understand what it is like to lose something, then it will be necessary to make him appreciate what it is that he is at risk of losing. What is it that a person shall miss when her freedom is trampled or stolen away from her. It is usually easy to show a person what they might feel if a concrete possession of theirs goes a'missing. As Professor Bruno Leoni has pointed out, it is always easier for the listener or reader to understand matters when we talk or write of material things, "we find it rather easy to be understood by our listeners. Should uncertainty arise about the meaning of our words, it would be sufficient, in order to eliminate the misunderstanding, simply to point to the thing we are naming or defining."

The principal difficulty is that freedom is a concept, not a percept; we cannot point to freedom or stick out our hand and feel it.[3]

Let us turn to David Hume, then John Stuart Mill:

> By liberty then we can only mean a power of acting or not acting, according to the determinations of the will; this is, if we choose to remain at rest, we may; if we choose to move, we also may.

> The only freedom which deserves the name, is that of pursuing our own good in our own way, so long as we do not attempt to deprive others of theirs, or impede their efforts to obtain it.

Note that we refer to the individual's possession of that precious right of freedom: I say individual. Freedom is a relative concept and can only be possessed by the individual: it cannot be possessed like a parcel of land, in common, by a group of people. An individual, either has freedom, or not. It was the French legal thinker Frédéric Bastiat who put his finger on this concept: "It is not the union of all liberties — liberty of conscience, of education, of association, of the press, of travel, of labor, of trade? In short, is not liberty the freedom of every person to make full use of his faculties, so long as he does not harm other persons while doing so?"

Thus, liberty be a state of being, where an individual is sovereign and answerable only to himself; where each is free to put at stake: his own life, his own well-being, his own time and his own property; where each, at all times, lives and acts as he wants within society at his own cost or to his own benefit, as the case may be; subject only and always to the restriction that an individual cannot proceed to act if that act clashes with or is in violation of the liberty of another.

The Necessity of Freedom:

> Liberty is not a means to a higher political end. It
> is itself the highest political end. — Lord Acton.

Freedom is not something we have gained through the efforts of our ancestors, but rather, it is something with which we are born, it comes with life's package. It is, as I have already asserted something that is necessary to our evolvement and is necessary to our continued involvement in life.

> It seems to me that this is theoretically right, for whatever the question under discussion — whether religious, philosophical, political, or economic; whether it concerns prosperity, morality, equality, right, justice, progress, responsibility, cooperation, property, labor, trade, capital, wages, taxes, population, finance, or government — at whatever point on the scientific horizon I begin my researches, I invariably reach this one conclusion: The solution to the problems of human relationships is to be found in liberty. ... all hope rests upon the free and voluntary actions of persons within the limits of right ...   — Bastiat.

In all of this, however, it is to be remembered, that we are all bound by the natural order of things. In the natural order of entities, there is no such thing as absolute freedom: each of us has his or her own master.

> He must have a master; but the master may be Nature or may be a fellow man. When he is under the impersonal coercion of Nature, we say that he is free; and when he is under the personal coercion of some one above him, we call him, according to the degree of his dependence, a slave, a serf, or a vassal.   — Spencer.

The Two Everlasting Empires:
Necessity & Free Will.

> Everywhere the human soul stands between a hemisphere of light and another of darkness; on the confines of the two everlasting empires, necessity and free will. — Thomas Carlyle.

To be free is no guarantee to life. One can be perfectly free as a castaway on an island: without food, water or shelter. One would be free, alright, and soon dead. But, I should add, one would be just as dead if one were in a land of plenty but tied down hand and foot to the ground. With freedom one is able to make his own way in the world, though the way may will lead to his destruction.

Freedom is the choice given, fundamentally, to act or not to act. But, in either event, one is bound to accept the consequences of his free choice. One has but little choice to go forth and to find food and seek shelter. The attending work and tribulation is not an encroachment on that person's freedom. The work and tribulation may be lessened, by a considerable amount, if people voluntarily collect themselves together into classes, usually as dictated by the laws of the natural economy.[4]

Freedom's Condition for Existence:

One of the lessons which the Durants left us was that "the freedom of individuals in society requires some regulation of conduct, the first condition of freedom is its limitation; make it absolute and it dies in chaos." We cannot have the freedom of each, flounder on the unlimited freedom of all.

Professor Hayek:

> The question then is how to secure the greatest possible freedom for all. This can be secured by uniformly restricting the freedom of all by abstract rules that preclude arbitrary or discriminatory coercion by or of other people, that prevent any from invading the free sphere of any other. In short, common concrete ends are replaced by common abstract rules. Government is needed only to enforce these abstract rules, and thereby to protect the individual against coercion, or invasion of his free sphere, by others. Whereas enforced obedience to common concrete ends is tantamount to slavery, obedience to common abstract rules (however burdensome they may still feel) provides scope for the most extraordinary freedom and diversity. Although it is sometimes supposed that such diversity brings chaos threatening the relative order that we also associate with civilization, it turns out that greater diversity brings greater order.

The grand goal is to maximize freedom. Freedom cannot exist by itself; it needs to be draped with the reins of constitutional and criminal laws. These laws, or "common abstract rules" as Hayek called them, will, in the nature of laws, take away freedom in their enforcement, but which are needed to "preclude arbitrary or discriminatory coercion by or of other people." Freedom should be such as to allow each person to pursue the objects of life, restrained only by the limits which the similar pursuits of their objects by other men impose. And, on the same point, I quote Canada's Stephen Leacock: "The further difficulty is added that everybody must act up to the rule or else nobody can. If all men are to be equal every man must know that the others will play their part towards him."

Criminal Law:

And so, we come to the subject of criminal law. Though open ended, criminal laws are to be limited in number. They are to be certain and only in negative form, such as not to kill, not to steal, not to commit assault, etc. Criminal law is to be defined in a careful manner in keeping with the wishes of the people and passed by more than a simple majority and to be within the confines of constitutional law. It is left to the citizens to set for themselves, through the workings of the common law, laws which will regulate civil proceedings (civil law: citizen/citizen v. criminal law: state/citizen).

More simply, as Bertrand Russell put it, criminal laws are "a method of enabling men to live together in a community in spite of the possibility that their desires may conflict." We each are free agents existing side by side, and through our family commitments and commercial contacts — whether conscious of it, or not — we mutually support one another. In a civilized society we function because we recognise invisible boundaries, within which boundaries individuals exist and operate. The boundaries are determined by both private and public law.

And so it is, we must have law, but in Benthan's declaration, "every law is evil, for every law is an infraction of liberty." So, while law might be necessary, it can be our undoing. As Lord Chesterfield was to observe to his fellows:

> One of the greatest Blessings we enjoy, one of the greatest Blessings a People, my Lords, can enjoy, is Liberty; but every Good in this Life has its alloy of Evil; Licentiousness is the Alloy of Liberty; it is an Ebullition, an Excrescence — it is a Speck upon the Eye of the Political Body, which I can never touch but with a

gentle — with a trembling Hand lest I destroy the Body, lest I injure the Eye upon which it is apt to appear. ... There is such a Connection between Licentiousness and Liberty, that it is not easy to correct the one, without dangerously wounding the other.

As to what our criminal laws should be? Well, each of us will develop our own unique list. Most of us will head up the list with the word murder and go from there — my list, I suspect, would be shorter than most. As one goes about making up his or her own list, he or she, should realize that each item (criminal law), added to the list, is just another cut, trenching into freedom: deeper and deeper.

To allow people to compete (within the confines of the criminal law) for all that they might need or want in this world: will mean, the preservation of freedom for every one. When people compete on the basis of their own personal skills and family connections, then they will be promoting a society in which most people will be able to carry on feeling satisfied that they, as least, fit in; or, where not, possess the feeling that they have the right to act, freely, again within the bounds of criminal law, strictly defined — so, as to effect change with the view to bringing some improvement to their lives. To proceed otherwise, to play favorites,[5] will lead to most every one feeling like misfits, and, what is more destructive, left with a feeling there is nothing that they, as individuals, can do about it. So, the question might be: do we wish to see a society where most every one fits in (some better than others), or a society that is crippled top to bottom with people who think they were really cut out for something better but see no means by which they might effect change, short of latching on to one or more of the demagogues that drift around in great numbers among us.

Freedom and the Law:

> Freedom consists in a people's being governed by laws
> made with their own consent.   — Swift.

It was a peculiar consequence of the Greek point of view that the individual as such was of no account as beside the state. We ourselves indeed, in our modern free democracies, think nothing so high, so noble as when the individual sacrifices his life for his country — the last supreme sacrifice. But the Greek point of view was something quite different. It meant that the individual had no rights that could not be sacrificed, by others, for the general welfare. We may pretend to such a view, but on real contact we shrink from it; the killing off of deformed children, putting idiots "out of the way," knocking old people on the head: fills us with instinctive horror. Even the painless killing of people hopelessly suffering before an inevitable death leaves us perplexed. The sanctity of human life "beats us out." To the Greek there was no problem in such things as these, and least of all to the Spartans, with whom the citizen's life was incased in an iron mould of authority. What the Greeks really cherished was the liberty and independence of their own little city-state.

The Destruction of Freedom:

> A child will weep a bramble's smart,
> A maid to see her sparrow part,
> A stribling for a woman's heart:
> But woo awaits a country, when
> She sees the tears of bearded men.
>   — Scott.

Put a frog into boiling water and he will immediately eject himself free of it; but content him, at first, in water of normal temperature and to gradually increase the temperature — why then you can boil him alive without restraint. In a speech to the Virginia Convention, on June the 16th, 1788, James Madison said: "I believe there are more instances of the abridgment of the freedom of the people by gradual and silent encroachments of those in power than by violent and sudden usurpations." Lurking dangers to our liberty exist, not only to "insidious encroachment," but, as Louis D. Brandeis, a much respected judge of the U. S. Supreme Court, pointed out, after echoing Madison's view, the greatest danger exists in "men of zeal, well-meaning but without understanding." (*Olmstead v. United States*.) More dangerous, still, is for the rest of us to fall asleep:

> Here, then, is the summation of the matter. We had thought, the decent people in all countries, that government by the people under democracy, and with it equal liberty for all, were things definitely achieved. We were forgetting the long struggle and the heroic sacrifice that gave them to the world. Bygone tyrannies and cruelties were forgotten in the nearer perspective of lesser things. Hence came a kind of inertia — a little slumber, a little sleep, a little folding of the hands to sleep — and thereby a creeping paralysis that made us almost let freedom slip from our hands.

Stephen Leacock wrote this in 1942, at a time when most all of Europe was under the Nazi boot. The Nazis did not spring with their racist policies full blown onto the stage; their atrocities were proceeded by a series of steps that took place over many years, steps that had the implicit consent of a sleepy people that were, are, no different than the rest of us.

"The Law."

> The history of law is the history of civilization, and law itself is only the blessed tie that binds human society together. ... Our long armed and hairy ancestors had no idea of redress beyond vengeance, or of justice beyond mere individual reprisal. ...
> The law, like everything we do and like everything we say, is a heritage from the past.
> — John Marshall Gest.

The Law and Civilization:

To state it in its extremes: Law is a cobweb,[1] entangling the weak, the sport of the strong. Most of those in the law however take the view of the author of our lead quote — Law is the very substance of civilization.[2] Implicit, in Judge Gest's comment about our "long armed and hairy ancestors" is the Hobbsian concept that man, in his natural state, is a vile beast that needs to be restrained by laws. Actually our western culture, as it has developed, took its cue from quite an opposite notion. While no doubt man must be restrained by laws, and indeed has been restrained by natural laws since his earliest beginnings, man is not, and could not, have come to be what he is today if he was but a snarling and thoughtless being who cannot see beyond his present place and moment in time.

The Age of Reason:

The enormous scientific and intellectual advancements made in the 17th century (*The Enlightenment* or *The Age of Reason*) brought about in Western Thought the age of the Scientific Man. The thinkers of the age were no

- 13 -

longer content to accept the cosmos and its contained life as a mystery to be simply accepted. The time had come for man to test his theories which flooded into his mind. To test these theories with his observations and to reset these theories in accordance with his accumulated observations. And, seemingly without end, to continue to re-test and to re-set.

> ... the closed and authoritarian system of the Middle Ages was replaced by the open and relativistic world of modern times. The closed geography of feudal Europe was pried open, first by the Crusades, then by the discovery of new trade routes, and finally by the world-wide explorations of the great navigators. The flat two-dimensional earth became a spheroid, three-dimensional world. The limited and static spatial theory of Ptolemy gave way to the dynamic heliocentric theory of Copernicus, Galileo, and Newton. Time, as well as space, was broadened. The development of chronology, the recovery of ancient monuments, and speculations about the future expanded the temporal scope of men's views. Economically, the closed and largely self-contained feudal estates were replaced by cities and towns, with the mutual interdependence that comes from the specialization of labor, till the whole medieval scheme of production was made over into the "free" system of commerce and industry.   — White.

It was Francis Bacon (1561-1626), much impressed by the materialist theories and the resultant discoveries of both Copernicus and Galileo delineating the principles of the inductive scientific method, who argued that the only knowledge of importance to man was empirically rooted in the natural world. (It is, incidentally, to Bacon we trace the expression, "Knowledge is Power.") The age had finally arrived whereby it was believed by a clear system of scientific inquiry, a new approach, that man might exercise mastery over the world. It was with such thinkers as did follow Bacon — Voltaire, Rousseau,

Montesquieu, Paine, and Jefferson — that this scientific approach was applied to political and social issues; and so arose the liberal, the humanitarian, and the belief in a sense of human progress and the belief that the state could be a rational instrument in bringing peace to the whole of society.[3]

John Locke:

Foremost among these new political thinkers was the Englishman, John Locke (1632-1704) who picked up on the beliefs of Bacon: "all knowledge is founded on and ultimately derives itself from sense ..." Locke, while insisting on the natural morality of pre-social man (unlike Hobbes who had espoused the view that man was a vile beast), thought it best for an individual to contract out "into civil society by surrendering personal power to the ruler and magistrates"; this, for Locke, was "a method of securing natural morality more efficiently." Thus we see stated the so-called *Social Contract Theory* which has been so badly misapplied and overly extended by political theorists. So too, it was Locke who wrote that if the "ruling body offends against natural law; it must be deposed." This was the philosophical stuff which sanctioned the rebellions of both the American colonialists in 1775, and the people of France in 1789. Incidentally, it is the political, legal and constitutional views of Locke which are at the core of all modern western democracies. All have been modelled after the first of them, the United States of America. The views of John Locke were carefully drafted into its Constitution of 1787.

Definition of Law:

Is it not my design, at this place, to show what stands as law, but rather my aim is to develop ideas on what law is.[4] Law is a "rule of conduct imposed by authority. ... The body of rules, whether proceeding from formal enactment or from custom, which a particular state or community recognizes as binding on its members or subjects." Upon considering this definition (*OED*), the first question that arises, is: "On whose authority?" Prior to the 18th century it was on the authority of a divinely appointed king; during the 18th and 19th centuries in England it was on the authority of the landed aristocracy[5]; in the 20th century it has been the people, in fact, I submit, the politicians who "manage" to get themselves elected[6]; now, having entered the 21st century, it's hard to say whose in charge, maybe no one, and maybe, that's the way it ought to be.

In considering the definition of law, we turn, once again to John Locke: "Law, in its proper Notion, is the Direction of a free and intelligent Agent to his proper Interest." "Proper Notion"? "Proper Interest"? What do you suppose Dr. Locke meant by this. My idea, is, that a proper Notion of law is that kind of law which comes from no human authority, other than from the individual person who is bound to follow it; it is the law that each of us carries around in our breast. A law is a rule which each of us, as a free and intelligent agent, will obey, because we fear the punishment that may come in the breaking of such law, and, by as much or more, because we fear the loss of respect from family and acquaintances. The "Proper Notion" of law is that which is found within a person, himself or herself; it is not imposed externally. In such a notion of law, there is absolutely no curtailment of that essential ingredient of life: "Freedom." The "Proper Notion" of law is that it is an ideal necessity given in the form of a precept, which we ought to follow.

For a further development of these ideas, it will be necessary for a person to understand that there are two basic kinds of law: one is scientific, or natural law; the other is a rule (or set of rules), apart from a natural law, which society prescribes for itself.

Natural Law:

Unlike man made law, which is prescriptive, natural law is descriptive. A person cannot break a natural law: it's unbreakable and that is a characteristic which defines it. It is unnecessary to take a natural rule (natural law) and make it into a man-made law; it is a complete waste of time and of resources to do so. Not to get too far into man-made law, a topic which I treat elsewhere ("On Legislation"), but only to help in defining natural law: a man-made law is to be distinguished from natural law in that it can be broken and this is because it is prescriptive law.

Natural law, natural justice, [is] the only standard by which any controversy whatever, between man and man, can be rightfully settled; being a principle whose protection every man demands for himself, whether he is willing to accord it to others, or not; being also an immutable principle, one that is always and everywhere the same, in all ages and nations; being self-evidently necessary in all times and places; being so entirely impartial and equitable towards all; so indispensable to the peace of mankind everywhere; so vital to the safety and welfare of every human being; being too, so easily learned, so generally known, and so easily maintained by such voluntary associations as all honest men can readily and rightfully form for that purpose. — Spooner.

Scientific law (natural law) is a "theoretical principle" deduced from particular facts as are gathered according to the sciences of observation, and is "applicable to a defined group or class of phenomena, and expressible by the statement that a particular phenomenon always occurs if certain conditions be present." (*OED*.) It is, as Blackstone said, "the laws of motion, of gravitation, of optics, or mechanics." It is, as Dr. Johnson described, "a fixed correspondence of cause and effect." They are laws that are derivatively obtained by watching the orderly sequences of Nature and applied to achieve a desired sequence of Nature. They are, as the English novelist George Meredith (1828-1909) described them, "Those firm laws Which we name Gods."

Let me give two examples of scientific law: Boyle's law, the principle, published by Robert Boyle (1627-1691), that the volume of a given mass of gas (the temperature being constant) varies inversely as the pressure. The second example is Charles's law, discovered by Alex. César Charles (1746-1823). For every degree centigrade of rise in temperature, the volume of a gas increases ... etc. There are many, many scientific laws, only some of which have been discovered. These are laws on which we daily depend and which, for the most part, we do not understand; we follow them; we do not question them.

Natural Law is a species of scientific law; it is a law implanted by nature on the human mind. Natural Law is a set of instinctual rules which we follow though we have no more understanding of them than we have of the great number of scientific laws on which we daily depend. These laws we regularly follow without the least understanding of them.

As it relates to man, it was the philosopher George Berkeley, who in 1712 said, "Self-preservation is the very first and fundamental law of nature." Thomas More, 1568, "The lawe of nature wylleth the mother to keepe the childe." Jeremy Bentham gave natural law a wider meaning than it in fact has when in 1780 he said, "Instead of the phrase, Law of Nature, you have sometimes Law of Reason."[7]

There was a time when natural law was profoundly revered, while conventional, legislated law hardly yet existed. It was a time when the common law[8] reigned supreme. As a preacher of the day would say: "The Lord endued Man with the Spirit of Understanding, by which he might be a Guide and Law unto himself." So, the principle that there is no need for men on high to lay laws down for the social organization of human kind, is a principle of long standing. There is absolutely nothing which has come out of the great social experiments of the 20th century to indicate to any well-informed person that this ancient principle need be different. Indeed, the results show that the principle of law as we are here dealing with (that there is no need for written laws in respect to social organization) is a principle firmly rooted in immutable law, natural law.

This subject of natural law — its existence and its extent — is a subject which fills a considerable number of shelves in any law school library. It should be sufficient, for now, to say, that if we can identify a body of positive principles and precepts which a good citizen cannot deny or ignore, then we have discovered natural law. With this discovery, we will begin to understand that there is a way to deal with the great social problems at hand without turning to intrusive man-made law.

Thomas Hobbes:

We need laws, so said Alexander Hamilton in 1788, because "the passions of men will not conform to the dictates of reason and justice without restraint." This of course expresses the Hobbesian view of human nature which we but only touched upon when Judge Gest was quoted at the first of this essay, viz. considering the propensities of our "long armed and hairy ancestors," laws are needed. It is well, even in this, an introduction to the subject of the law, to fix firmly upon the thoughts of Thomas Hobbes if one is to consider if there is a need for man-made laws, and if so, to what extent.

The Englishman, Thomas Hobbes (1588-1679) wrote a book in 1651, *Leviathan*. This book has been described as the "greatest, perhaps the sole, masterpiece of political philosophy in the English language." It is a treatise on the origin and ends of government. It was Hobbes' view that while man's nature does not require a governing state, independent of his own, a better life might well be assured through the existence of an outside governing state; it was unnatural[9] for man to put himself under the control of others, to have a government, but that it was rational to do so. Both Hobbes and Locke ended up in the same place, viz. a government and system of law is best, but where Hobbes and Locke differed — and it is important to understand this — is in the reasons why man ought to put himself under external government. For Locke, it was just that man would be better off under government, but in coming to this conclusion Locke did not cast man as a vile beast to be reined in. Hobbes, on the other hand, was of the view that if man were not brought under a system of government and laws, then man would proceed to lead his life in the midst of others all being singularly driven by an egotistical psychology, and thus, life for most would be "nasty, brutish and short, a constant war of every man with every man." Rational, enlightened self-interest, so the Hobbesian theory goes, makes men want to escape such a predicament by the establishment of a contract in which they surrender power to an absolute sovereign, whose commands are the law; freedom being relegated to the spheres not covered by the sovereign's commands. This arrangement is binding only so long as the sovereign has power to enforce it. To put this theory in a modern context, this arrangement, if it is to work, will work whether sovereignty is vested in a person, or an assembly of persons. It is, to be clear, the Hobbesian view that the first principle of human behavior was egoism, or self-interest, and it was this egoism, that was the root of all social conflict. The primitive individualism as described by Thomas Hobbes is a myth. The savage was not, and could not have been, solitary; his instinct was and is collectivist.[10] The rules of human conduct gradually evolved, particularly the rules governing the possession and exchange of property, viz. contract law. These rules were handed down by tradition, teaching and imitation, and consisted largely of prohibitions, that is to say law evolved to be restrictive in nature.

The human species like every life form, indeed like the cosmos in which life exists, evolved through a massive period of time. Darwinian theory, now the accepted theory as to our origins, to be fair to Hobbes, is a theory of modern times. In spite of the images, over the thousands and thousands of years just preceding civilization, the cave man could not have been much different than any man we might observe as exists on earth today. Certainly it cannot be expected that the observations that one might make of a "cave man," of say 100,000 years back, could be any more different than the observations that the same person might make of a randomly picked man of the 21st century. (Unfortunately, lacking a time machine, we are unable to put the matter to the test.) Putting aside a divinity theory — which, at any rate, must necessarily take us outside of scientific parameters — if the dark and gloomy Hobbesian view of man is to be accepted, then what must occur is an adequate explanation as to how man came to be — by and large — the caring, thinking and beauty appreciating creature that indeed he has come to be. Locke accepted that man, while far from being angelic, nonetheless, had a wonderful nature and that a government and laws were desirable so as to extent man's horizons. However, in order not to dampen down the very thing that through the eons formed him — his freedom of action — it is necessary to impose but the simplest set of laws which would achieve the objective, "bringing peace to the whole of society." Criminal law of a practical nature is needed to deal (I favor the word punish) with the offensive actors amongst us (including government, but more on that in a moment). What is permissible, in a proper notion of a government and a system of laws, is to allow government, and only government, as an agent of the people, to use force against another, but even then, only if it is against an offensive person where the offenses have been carefully spelt out before hand (criminal law). In order to achieve this end, "social peace," on strict Lockian theory, it would only be necessary to set up government for its principal goals (and maybe only goals) of the punishment of criminals and the enforcement of the law which people have set for themselves (tort law, contract law; or, more generally, the common law). In setting up the mechanisms of government, the prime consideration is to be the control of its (government) power. Laws beyond that which is needed to achieve the goal of "social peace" are not necessary, and, indeed, are harmful in that they would impede man's progress by infringing that which sustains life: Freedom. In the final analysis, according to the Lockian view of society, not much is required to be done by government; society is quite capable of taking care of itself.

Rule of Law:

While philosophers will argue its extent, few will take issue with the need for law and that it is to have universal application: I now write of the all important legal notion, The Rule of Law.

The subject of power: what it is and how it is wielded is a subject I treat in my essay, "On Government." Enough to say that power, for the purposes of this introductory monograph on the law, as Lord Acton pointed out, corrupts and in turn is misused; this is especially so when power is concentrated in the hands of a few, as it is in government. It was the French philosopher, Montesquieu — having spent time in England studying its political system, and, in particular, the writings of Locke — who wrote, in his work, *The Spirit of Laws* (1748), that it was a necessity, in any proper constitution of a country, to compartmentalize the power of government. A written demonstration of Montesquian doctrine, the separation of powers, exists in the American Constitution. The framers of which, before setting quill to parchment, struggled much and understood very well the inherent danger of government power.

The idea behind Montesquieu's doctrine is to prevent a tyrant from taking control by the use of the power that we have intentionally concentrated in the hands of our agents, those who run the government. Such power, so the doctrine goes, must be distributed to three groups of persons: those who make the law, those who enforce the law, and those who oversee the first two groups. Thus we have three branches of government wielding power: legislative, executive and judicial. In their functions, each is to be separated from the others. And, essentially, each group, as are all citizens, are subject to the same law, in the same way: this we have come to know as the Rule of Law.

Conclusions:

Thus, we have considered the origins of the law; its nature; its various kinds; and its application. We have seen that law is more than just the expression of the conscious will of a king or of a legislator, indeed, if such expressions run against natural law, against natural justice, then such expressions may not be law at all. We have seen that the law which governs society, has, at its very roots, evolved as a result of natural forces arising through the interaction of people. As Cardozo has lectured, "nature had imprinted in us, as one of the very elements of reason ... that law springs from relations of fact which exist between things."[11] Thus, I submit, that all law is traceable to only one: The Law of Cause and Effect. Given certain factors the same motives always produce the same actions; the same events follow from the same causes. It is this single law, that, in the final analysis, comes to our assistance when we are put to the most difficult task of predicting the behavior of our fellow human beings. Each person is obliged to make their own prediction of future events and govern themselves accordingly.

It is universally acknowledged that there is a great uniformity among the actions of men, in all nations and ages, and that human nature remains still the same, in its principles and operations. The same motives always produce the same actions: the same events follow from the same causes. Ambition, avarice, self-love, vanity, friendship, generosity, public spirit: these passions, mixed in various degrees, and distributed through society, have been, from the beginning of the world, and still are, the source of all the actions and enterprises, which have ever been observed among mankind.

— David Hume.

"The Common Law."

The law is wiser than cabal or interest.
— Edmund Burke, 1794.

Mastering the lawless science of
our law ... That codeless myriad of
precedent, That wilderness of single
instances ...   — Tennyson.

Common law is law that comes from the common people, versus legislation which comes from the "experts."

Common law comes about at the root levels of society: it is not law that is imposed by some authority from on high. The development of common law was essentially a private affair concerning millions of people throughout dozens of generations and stretching across several centuries. It is a process that is self adjusting and which goes on everyday unnoticed, without great expense to the state and with out fractionalizing society. This is to be compared to the legislative process, a comparison made in my essay, "On Legislation."

Before getting into the specifics of the common law, let me first set forth a small speech given in 1875 by an obscure judge. The name of the judge was The Honorable Joseph Neilson, Chief Justice of the City Court of Brooklyn. He gave this address at some sort of a gathering (I don't think in his courtroom). The publisher of the book (*A Collection of Arguments and Speeches by Eminent Lawyers*) in which I discovered this short speech, entitled it "The Growth of Principles."

At the sea shore you pick up a pebble, fashioned after a law of nature, in the exact form that best resists pressure, and worn as smooth as glass. It is so perfect that you take it as a keepsake. But could you know its history from the time when a rough fragment of rock fell from the overhanging cliff into the sea, to be taken possession of by the under currents, and dragged from one ocean to another, perhaps around the world, for a hundred years, until in reduced and perfect form it was cast upon the beach as you find it, you would have a fit illustration of what many principles, now in familiar use, have endured, thus tried, tortured and fashioned during the ages. We stand by the river and admire the great body of water flowing so sweetly on; could you trace it back to its source, you might find a mere rivulet, but meandering on, joined by other streams and by secret springs, and fed by the rains and dews of heaven, it gathers volume and force, makes its way through the gorges of the mountains, plows, widens and deepens its channel through the provinces, and attains its present majesty. Thus it is that our truest systems of science had small beginnings, gradual and countless contributions, and finally took their place in use, as each of you, from helpless childhood and feeble boyhood, have grown to your present strength and maturity. No such system could be born in a day. It was not as when nature in fitful pulsations of her strength suddenly lifted the land into mountain ranges, but rather, as with small accretions, gathered in during countless years, she builds her islands in the seas.

It took a long time to learn the true nature and office of governments; to discover and secure the principles commonly indicated by such terms as 'Magna Charta,' the 'Bill of Rights,' 'Habeas Corpus,' and the 'Right of trial by jury;' to found the family home, with its laws of social order, regulating the rights and duties of each member of it, so that the music at the domestic hearth might flow on without discord; the household gods so securely planted that 'Though the wind and the rain might enter, the king could not'; to educate noise into music, and music into melody; to infuse into the social code and into the law a spirit of Christian charity, something of the benign temper of the New Testament, so that no man could be persecuted for conscience sake, so that there should be an end of human sacrifice for mere faith or opinion; the smouldering fires at the foot of the stake put out, now, thank God, as effectually as if all the waters that this night flood the rivers had been poured in upon them. It took a long time to learn that war was a foolish and cruel method of settling international differences as compared with arbitration; to learn that piracy was less profitable than a liberal commerce; that unpaid labor was not as good as well-requited toil; that a splenetic old woman, falling into trances and shrieking prophecies, was a fit subject for the asylum rather than to be burned as a witch.

It took a long, long time after the art of printing had been perfected before we learned the priceless value, the sovereign dignity and usefulness of a free press.

But these lessons have been taught and learned; taught for the most part by the prophets of our race, men living in advance of their age, and understood only by the succeeding generations. But you have the inheritance.

The common law is a great scientific lab, the resources and results of which are brought to bear on the populations which are fortunate enough to possess an English common law tradition such as exists, for example, in such countries as Canada, the United States and Australia. Nature is the great and ultimate scientific testing lab and it always, in time, shakes out the truth. Whether we appreciate it, or not, for hundreds of years: the common law tests, observes, adjusts and re-observes on a continual bases.[1]

The fact of the matter is that there exists all around us a great body of law which has not ever been (nor could it be) written down in one spot. In a way, it's, it's more of a process which has a single guiding rule, the "golden rule," a negative rule: "Don't do something to someone that you don't want to have visited on yourself, either directly or through the agency of a government." Though it has suffered much at the hands of legislators, common law is yet followed in all major English speaking nations around the world. Common law to England was and is its very force. The greatness of England, certainly in the past, is attributable, I would say fully attributable, to the stabilizing and enriching institution that we have come to know as common law. This subject of the common law is a great and wonderful subject: its evolutionary development and its great benefits make it the most superior law system known in the world, as history will readily tell.

The common law is as a result of a natural sequence which hardened first into custom and then into law. It did not come about as an act of will, as an act of some group aware only of the instant moment, unaware of the nature and history of man. It came about as a result of a seamless and continual development, through processes we can hardly begin to understand; it evolved along with man.

If we were to take the common law, figuratively speaking as a huge tent and net, so to cover and hold safe all those engaged in the human circus, we may liken the guys or supporting lines to tradition and culture.

Tradition:

> There is hardly an absurdity of the past that cannot be found flourishing somewhere in the present.
> — Durant.

It was a Dutch meteorologist who lived back in the 19th century and who formulated a law in respect to wind known as Buys-Ballot's Law of the Winds. It is expressed as follows:

The wind neither blows round the space of lowest pressure in circles returning on themselves, nor does it blow directly towards that space; but it takes a direction intermediate, approaching, however, more nearly to the direction and course of circular curves than of radii to a centre.

Thus expressed, it is hard for most of us mortals to understand what this Dutchman, Buys-Ballot, was talking about. How about this —

... if a man stands with his back to the wind, the lower pressure will be to his left in the northern hemisphere, and to his right in the southern.

Ah! Now, we are making some progress. In Nova Scotia, the prevailing direction of our weather systems is north-east, that is to say we generally get what's coming to us from the south-west, up the eastern American seaboard. In Nova Scotia, if one were to stand with his back to the Atlantic ocean and where, at the same time, one's back is to the wind, then the low (bad weather) is to the south-west and heading for you; with the wind just the opposite (blowing off shore), then the low is to the north-west and heading away from you. A flat ocean with an offshore wind is something that a weather-fearing fisherman in Nova Scotia likes. He knows nothing of Buys-Ballot's Law of the Winds, but he obeys it; he knows about it in his gut; and knows — Oh! So, well — the grief that will come to him and his family if he does not obey The Law of the Winds.

Primitive man knew nothing of laws, all he knew was custom. Custom, or tradition, evolved into rules for living. They grew spontaneously, viz. not deliberately designed by some particular human mind. While no one can point to the origins of our traditional moral rules, their function in human society is clear enough. These moral rules, or traditions, are necessary to preserve the existing state of affairs; such that culture was allowed to evolve; and in turn, with culture, civilizations came about. Thus, as David Hume wrote, man developed in an evolutionary fashion — not only biologically, but also culturally. That, like the lot of all animals, man evolved in accordance with certain natural rules, in that "no form can persist unless it possesses those powers and organs necessary for its subsistence: some new order or economy must be tried and so on, without intermission; until at last some order which can support and maintain itself, is fallen upon."

The preservation of existing laws as was represented by traditions and cultural rules, at least to early man, was of greater concern than putting up with bad laws: change was what men feared: change and its social upheaval was what brought on suffering and death. I quote from Bagehot's work:

In early societies it matters much more that the law should be fixed than that it should be good. Any law which the people of ignorant times enact is sure to involve many misconceptions, and to cause many evils. Perfection in legislation is not to be looked for, and is not, indeed, much wanted in a rude, painful, confined life. But such an age covets fixity. That men should enjoy the fruits of their labour, that the law of property should be known, that the law of marriage should be known, that the whole course of life should be kept in a calculable track, is the *summum bonum* of early ages, the first desire of semi-civilized mankind. In that age men do not want to have their laws adapted, but to have their laws steady. The passions are so powerful, force so eager, the social bond so weak, that the august spectacle of an all but unalterable law is necessary to preserve society. In the early stages of human society all change is thought an evil. And most change is an evil. The conditions of life are so simple and so unvarying that any decent sort of rules suffice, so long as men know what they are. Custom is the first check on tyranny; that fixed routine of social life at which modern innovations have, and by which modern improvement is impeded, is the primitive check on base power. The perception of political expediency has then hardly begun; the sense of abstract justice is weak and vague; and a rigid adherence to the fixed mould of transmitted usage is essential to an unmarred, unspoiled, unbroken life.

Stare Decisis:

This idea, as expressed by Bagehot, is picked up in the law as it exists today. When a court decides a case it does so on the merits of the case before it. The court's decision is meant to only effect the rights of the parties, the litigants, before it. The court, however, is obliged to apply settled principles of law. The decision of any respected court amounts to a recap of the law needed to resolve the case before it. The law as it is used in the particular case has a universal applicability to all future cases embracing similar facts, and involving the same or analogous principles. These decisions, many being years and years old, thus became statements of law, to be applied by all courts when measuring the private and public rights of citizens. It is this stream of cases, within the arc of the great pendulum of time, which changes the banks of the law: the common law, thus, as it turns out, is a living, creeping, creature.

Do not, however, be mistaken — there, is, a conscious effort by those involved (lawyers and judges) to keep the law pure: not to change it, but to apply it. This principle is called *stare decisis*, Latin, which literally translated means, "stand by things decided." *Stare decisis* has come to us as a most sacred rule of law. A judge is to apply the law as it is presented to him through the previous decisions of the court; it is not the judge's function to make or remake the law. However, judges do make law even though they try not to; indeed it is their function, under a system of common law, to do so; but not consciously and only over the course of time, many years, as numerous similar cases are heard and decided. The common law has been built up like pearls in an oyster, slowly and always in response to some small personal aggravation, infinitesimal layer after infinitesimal layer. It is built by the adjudications of courts:

> ... built up as it has been by the long continued and arduous labors, grown venerable with years, and interwoven as it has become with the interests, the habits, and the opinions of the people. [Without the common law a court would] in each recurring case, have to enter upon its examination and decision as if all were new, without any aid from the experience of the past, or the benefit of any established principle or settled law. Each case with its decision being thus limited as law to itself alone, would in turn pass away and be forgotten, leaving behind it no record of principle established, or light to guide, or rule to govern the future.
>
> — *Hanford v. Archer*, 4 Hill, 321.

Tyrants can only get a hold of a central system where the rules issue from a single authority (government); tyrants cannot get a hold of a system which depends on a spontaneous participation in the law-making process on the part of each and all of the inhabitants of a country, viz. a system of common law.

———————————

"On Legislation."

> They have but few laws ...
> but they think it against all
> right and justice that men
> should be bound to these
> laws, which either be in
> number more than be able
> to read, or else blinder and
> darker than that any man
> can well understand them.
> — From More's *Utopia.*

What is Legislation?

Though I hate to give it a place in the scheme of things, legislation, I suppose, falls as one of two heads of law. First is the common law, the sweetheart at the head of the table who gets things done by consent and agreement; and then, at the other end, smelly and brutish, with sword and rope, sits legislation and claims its right to a position at the table because it fits the definition of the larger concept of law: "A rule of conduct imposed by authority. ... The body of rules, whether proceeding from formal enactment or from custom, which a particular state or community recognizes as binding on its members or subjects." (*OED.*) However, legislation is always subject to losing its authority as law by slipping out from under the definition; and this, on account of its despicable character. Legislation will lose its force as being law when a significant part of the community does not and will not recognize legislation (for whatever reason) as being binding upon itself.

The Object of Legislation:

A person or group of persons, surprisingly easily, can make another or others do what is wanted. One way is by negotiation and accommodation, viz. by contract, that is to say, to trade with them. Another way is to command that which is desired to be done and back it up with the threat of brute physical force: that is to use coercion: that is what we call legislative law: that is the dark side of the law.

Let me turn to Leslie Stevenson, "a reader in logic and Metaphysics at the University of St. Andrews, Scotland" who states, fairly, the object of legislation:

> The object of our legislation is not the welfare of any particular class, but of the whole community. It uses persuasion or force to unite all citizens and make them share together the benefits which each individually can confer on the community; and its purpose in fostering the attitude is not to enable every one to please himself, but to make each man a link in the unity of the whole.

The definition of legislation and the nature of its object, will be best understood by going back to its historical origins.

The Origins of Legislation:

The word legislation is derived from the Latin words standing for "law" and "bringing." A quick check of the *OED* reveals that originally the word had more of a religious meaning than anything else, in that an act of legislation was an act of a high priest revealing a Divine Law. Today we understand that legislation consists of sets of rules which a majority of legislators, sitting in their chamber, declare to be laws; which, as such, become enforceable through the coercive power of the state.

Today, and for some time now, these rules have been printed up and bound into books, statute books. Before the days of solemn legislatures it was not thought necessary to write laws down in any one place, indeed, legislation, as I have just explained, did not much exist before the creation of the first legislatures. It never did fill any prominent place among the duties of a king.

Originally the principal function of the legislature was to control the power of the king. They did this by controlling the supply of money for the needs of the crown. Thus, in its earlier day the legislature was an overseer of the power of the crown. It restricted its law making activities to that of making rules for itself, and of course, rules as to what trading commodities were to be taxed. Prior to the passing of *The Great Reform Bill of 1832* by the British parliament, little thought was given to improve the state of society by the use of legislation. Indeed, it would be difficult to point to much positive social legislation passed, prior to the arrival of the 20th century.

In the late 19th century we see examples of legislative efforts to codify the existing law. *The Infant's Relief Act* of *1874* was but a declaration or publication of the common law development that an infant's contract is voidable at the infant's option. The same can be said of the *Sale of Goods Act* of *1893*, and the *Law of Property Act of 1925* (in most of its aspects). These were legislative attempts to sort out the apparent higgledy-piggledy status of the common law. This was an innocent start; but all lamentable situations which lodge themselves, inextricable it seems, usually make their appearance with an innocent start. In the western democracies the social engineers were given a full head, particularly after

WWII, and the quantity of meddlesome legislation picked up in an exponential manner and continued over a forty year period, or so; and only in the last decade, have we seen, as the huge social bills began rolling in, some reversal of a process which was tapping out the two essentials ingredients of social activity (no matter the kind): incentive and liberty.

The Legislative Process: Piecemeal v. Holistic:

If our elected representatives proceeded properly, then they would pass fewer laws and should be much the busier for it. I do not question that part of the legislators' job is to pass rules (legislation) that they and the rest of us are bound to obey, but the enactment of legislation is a ceremonial proceeding which takes place at the very end of what should be a very painstaking process. It is not the legislator's job, nor is it possible, to come up with a grand social design. The approach to the serious business of law making has long since been established. There are rules.[1] These rules are to govern those charged with the task, and they must during the entire process constantly keep the object of the exercise in mind. The rules first call for a careful defining of the terms. Then the rules allow for a change in the law only where it can be demonstrated that the change would not only effectively deal with the social evils to be got at, but shown to be free from greater evils. Further, in addition, any new legislation proposed should be consistent with existing law.

This business of passing laws can only be done on a "piecemeal" basis, it is, as I have already pointed out, not possible to come up with a grand social design. The philosopher, Karl Popper in his work *The Poverty of Historicism*, dealt with the point:

The piecemeal engineer [as opposed to the 'holistic' or 'Utopian engineer'] knows like Socrates, how little he knows. He knows that we can learn only from our mistakes. Accordingly, he will make his way, step by step, carefully comparing the results expected with the results achieved, and always on the look-out for the unavoidable unwanted consequences of any reform; and he will avoid undertaking reforms of a complexity and scope which make it impossible for him to disentangle causes and effects, and to know what he is really doing. ...

The holists reject the piecemeal approach as being too modest. Their rejection of it, however, does not quite square with their practice; for in practice they always fall back on a somewhat haphazard and clumsy although ambitious and ruthless application of what is essentially a piecemeal method without its cautious and self-critical character. The reason is that, in practice, the holistic method turns out to be impossible; the greater the holistic changes attempted, the greater are their unintended and largely unexpected repercussions, forcing upon the holistic engineer the expedient of piecemeal *improvization*. In fact, this expedient is more characteristic of centralized or collectivistic planning than of the more modest and careful piecemeal intervention; and it continually leads the Utopian engineer to do things which he did not intend to do; that is to say, it leads the notorious phenomenon of *unplanned planning*. ...

It seems to escape the well-meaning Utopianist that this programme implies an admission of failure, even before he launches it. For it substitutes for his demand that we build a new society, fit for men and women to live in, the demand that we 'mould' these men and women to fit into his new society. This, clearly, removes any possibility of testing the success or failure of the new society. For those who do not like living in it only admit thereby that they are not yet fit to live in it; that their 'human impulses' need further 'organizing'. But without the possibility of tests, any claim that a 'scientific' method is being employed evaporates. The holistic approach is incompatible with a truly scientific attitude.

The socialists[2] of the age saw legislation as a way of re-making society; a way of curing social ills; a way to balance things; a way to dispense and bring into force "the pure word of Liberalism." With the conclusion of the Second World War, the bureaucracies as a result thereof being well in place, the politicians got down to serious business and legislative schemes of all varieties were hatched and put in place.[3]

Legislation: Robbers' Rules:

What, then, is legislation? It is an assumption by one man, or body of men, of absolute, irresponsible dominion over all other men whom they can subject to their power. It is the assumption by one man, or body of men, of a right to subject all other men to their will and their service. It is the assumption by one man, or body of men, of a right to abolish outright all the natural rights, all the natural liberty of all other men; to make all other men their slaves; to arbitrarily dictate to all other men what they may, and may not, do; what they may, and may not have; what they may, and may not, be. It is, in short, the assumption of a right to banish the principle of human rights, the principle of justice itself, from off the earth, and set up their own personal will, pleasure, and interest in its place. All this, and nothing less, is involved in the very idea that there can be any such thing as human legislation that is obligatory upon those upon whom it is imposed.   — Lysander Spooner.

Spooner was of the view that there is only one universal obligation: to keep the peace. He was of the view that this was one simple law that all are bound to keep or be penalized by the others as represented by the State. The general observance of such a law means people hurt no one and leave others to collect what is their due. Why is it that this simple model is not at all reflected in reality. The answer is because there are robbers in the world, people who would rather loot than work. Robbers are usually easy to identify. All one can do is to try to stay out of the path of robbers, or, better yet, find and join the strongest robber group in your neighborhood.

Robber groups became stronger, and bigger, and increased their power by uniting with each other and perfecting their organizations. Peace treaties among robber groups were struck and broken depending on whether a power equilibrium existed, or not. "All the great governments of the world ... have been of this character. ... their laws, as they have called them, have only such agreements as they have found it necessary to enter into, in order to maintain their organizations ..."

All these laws have had no more real obligation than have the agreements which brigands, bandits, and pirates find it necessary to enter into with each other, for the more successful accomplishment of their crimes, and the more peaceable division of their spoils. ...

Thus the whole business of legislation, which has now [mid 19th century] grown to such gigantic proportions, had its origin in the conspiracies, which have always existed among the few, for the purpose of holding the many in subjection, and extorting from them their labor, and all the profits of their labor.

And the real motives and spirit which lie at the foundation of all legislation — notwithstanding all the pretenses and disguises by which they attempt to hide themselves — are the same to-day as they always have been. The whole purpose of this legislation is simply to keep one class of men in subordination and servitude to another.   — Spooner.

We should not optimize against the imaginable, and certainly not against the impossible; at times we might try to deal with the probable. There are no limits to most people's imagination, and if they are given access to people's pockets — why, then, these dreamers will see no limits in respect on how "we" are to cure the problems they perceive. Think of it: if we were to design all of our policies around the worst thing that could possibly happen, then, what kind of world will we have. If our objective is that each of us should proceed in absolute safety in that which we do, we will, each of us, have to be locked up in our respective cubical and put under twenty-hour surveillance. Absolute safety can be achieved only if liberty of movement is absolutely forbidden. Each of us will have to be told (by whom or who, we might wonder) not only what we cannot do, but what we can do. The relationship of the governors and those governed will be, as Frédéric Bastiat observed, as that which exists between "the clay and the potter." Such people, as Bastiat further observed, do not "recognize a principle of action in the heart of man — and a principle of discernment in man's intellect." People do not go around purposely trying to do themselves or their neighbors harm, nor do they normally proceed in their affairs in a negligent manner (and, if they did, there is a remedy to the injured person at law). It seems, if "the legislators left persons free to follow their own inclinations, they would arrive at atheism instead of religion, ignorance instead of knowledge, property instead of production and exchange." It is a wrong idea, but as Bastiat wrote: "Open at random any book on philosophy, politics, or history, and you will probably see how deeply rooted in our country is this idea — the child of classical studies, the mother of socialism."

Legislation always proceeds on the false notion that the majority is in the right. The only thing a majority has for sure, is the power to sweep away the rights of the minority. A wrong idea is a wrong idea no matter how many should want to believe it. History has proven, time and time again, that those who believe in the right idea are often in the minority.

Professor Bruno Leoni:

Whereas scientific and technological results are always due to relatively small minorities or particular individuals, often, if not always, in opposition to ignorant or indifferent majorities, legislation, especially today, always reflects the will of a contingent majority within a committee of legislators who are not necessarily more learned or enlightened than the dissenters. Where authorities and majorities prevail, as in legislation, individuals must yield, regardless of whether they are right or wrong. ...

Too many vested interests and too many prejudices are obviously ready to defend the inflation of the legislative process in contemporary society. However, unless I am wrong, everybody will be confronted sooner or later with the problem of a resulting situation that seems to promise nothing but perpetual unrest and general oppression.

What is better: the living law of the people, common law; or, legislation enacted by the "representatives" of the people. The plain truth is, that the collectivists in our midst, would like to have their ideas written up as legislation and thus to bind us all to their particular philosophy. The process is at the general expense, and often to no one's benefit except those who are running the program.

Certainty of Law:

One of the principal reasons given by those who advocate legislation is that with legislation the population will have, to a better degree, certainty of law. It is necessary, if a person is to plan their affairs, that he or she knows what the law says about the particular activity that is being contemplated. We see from a study of the history of law that this element, certainty of the law, has ranked high in the mind of the juridic thinker. The

Greeks wrote their laws on the walls of public buildings; we should do no less, than writing them out in statute books. Supporters of legislation argue that judge made law[4] is too uncertain and can only be found by persons versed in legal research, in dusty old case reports.

The truth of the matter is, that written law, is more uncertain than judge made law, the common law. And the reason for that, is, it is simpler to change written law than the common law. Common law is a slow moving, evolutionary sort of thing; it is not under the command of any single generation. As experience has proven, anyone of us can go to bed one night with one set of legislative laws and wake up the next morning with an entirely different set. One set of laws are passed to cure a perceived problem. After some time, assuming the problem has been relieved (often there is no effect, indeed the problem to be got at can become even worse on account of the legislation) other problems are brought on directly related to the implementation of the "curing" legislation. So, more legislation is rushed in to fix the additional problems. And so, it is not unusual to see certain legislation to be written and rewritten over and over. This is a separate and inherent problem: the jerkiness in legislation. Judges, on the whole, are scholarly individuals who are interested in ascertaining things rather than, like legislators, changing things. So too, unlike legislators, judges cannot easily enact arbitrary rules of their own; we needn't expect sudden laws from judges as we have come to expect from legislators with their wide ranging and imperious manner.

Walter Bagehot, a much respected English legal writer, wrote about this inherent jerkiness in legislation:

The manner of our legislation is indeed detestable, and the machinery for settling that manner odious. A committee of the whole House, dealing, or attempting to deal, with the elaborate clauses of a long Bill, is a wretched specimen of severe but misplaced labour. It is sure to wedge some clause into the Act, such as that which the judge said 'seemed to have fallen by itself, perhaps, from heaven, into the mind of the legislature', so little had it to do with anything on either side or around it. At such times government by a public meeting displays its inherent defects, and is little restrained by its necessary checks.

Thus, certainty of the law is best served where there exists a series of rules spontaneously adopted by people in common and eventually ascertained by judges through centuries and generations, and not from imprecise text emanating from legislatures which are driven by groups who know little about the "evil" which they see and would like to get at.

The Common Will:

Another of the arguments of those who advocate the extensive use of legislation is that it is through legislation that the will of the people, the common will, might be expressed. Common will is a vaporous phantasm in an ideologue's head. The common will is not something that exists in real life, any more than any kind of an average exists in real life. "... nobody is more competent to know what one's will is than one is oneself." (Leoni.) Thus, we must, as much as possible, leave the decision making process at the level which will satisfy the most numbers, viz. at the level of the people themselves — hiring "experts" to conjure up what it is the people want on the basis of something that does not exist, the common will, is both expensive and fruitless.

... a 'common' will, that is, a will that may be presumed as existent in all citizens, but to the expression of the particular will of certain individuals and groups who were lucky enough to have a contingent majority of legislators on their side at a given moment.
— Leoni.

The common will — again, if it can be identified at all — will be identified in a negative sense, not in a positive sense. Survey any randomly selected group of people and it will likely be found, and then only in its simplest terms, a commonality as to what it is they do not want; there will be a great diversity as to want they do want. Thus, reasonable persons might agree on what it is they do not want to see happen within their community. Criminal law (the state versus the person) and the law of tort (the person versus the person) evolved because there are forms of behavior which will generally not be tolerated in a community. Elaborate, positive, legislation is not necessary to keep the peace; nor, I assert, will such legislation cure injustice which certain people perceive exists in society; indeed, such legislation, is, I further assert, on a separate head, inherently unjust.

The common will can only be had by a survey of the market of ideas, including legal ideas. Common law, by its nature is in fact an ongoing survey, and more than that — it in time identifies the legal problems and brings a specific remedy tailored to the aggrieved party, and not much at the general expense. It is a myth that in a collectivist system the law passing body is guided by the common will. A country which attempts to set itself up extensively under legislative law, at the expense of common law, is like a country in which all the relevant decisions are made by a handful of directors, whose knowledge of the whole situation is fatally limited and whose respect, if any, for the people's wishes is subject to that limitation. As Leoni points out, there is more than an analogy between the market economy and common law, "just as there is much more than an analogy between a planned economy and legislation."

We all seem to make the assumption that, somehow, legislators not only know how to cure a particular social problem; but that they understand, in the first place, what the problem, or rather what the antecedents of the problem are. "Social scientists" do not have the power to follow out in thought, with any correctness, the sequences of even simple phenomena, much less those of a more complex nature such as those which societies display. It would be to our considerable advantage, in these circumstances, to restrict these "social scientists" in their interferences with the natural state of things. Herbert Spencer, in his usual precise manner, put his finger on the difficult problems that face our elective representatives when it comes to exercising "legislative judgment":

> The decision is one of those small holes through which a wide prospect may be seen, and a disheartening prospect it is. In a very simple case there is here displayed a scarcely credible inability to see how much effect will follow so much cause; and yet the business of the assembly exhibiting this inability is that of dealing with causes and effects of an extremely involved kind. All the processes going on in society arise from the concurrences and conflicts of human actions, which are determined in their nature and amounts by the human constitution as it now is — are as much results of natural causation as any other results, and equally imply definite quantitative relations between causes and effects. Every legislative act presupposes a diagnosis and a prognosis; both of them involving estimations of social forces and the work done by them. Before it can be remedied, an evil must be traced to its source in the motives and ideas of men as they are, living under the social conditions which

exist — a problem requiring that the actions tending toward the result shall be identified, and that there shall be something like a true idea of the quantities of their effects as well as the qualities. A further estimation has then to be made of the kinds of degrees of influence that will be exerted by the additional factors which the proposed law will set in motion: what will be the resultants produced by the new forces co-operating with pre-existing forces — a problem still more complicated than the other.

We are quite prepared to hear the unhesitating reply, that men incapable of forming an approximately true judgement on a matter of simple physical causation may yet be very good law-makers. So obvious will this be thought by most, that a tacit implication to the contrary will seem to them absurd; and that it will seem to them absurd is one of the many indications of the profound ignorance that prevails. It is true that mere empirical generalizations which men draw from their dealings with their fellows suffice to give them some ideas of the proximate effects which new enactments will work. Seeing these, they think they see as far as needful. Discipline in physical science, however, would help to show them the utter inadequacy of calculating consequences based on simple data. And if there needs proof that calculations of consequences so based are inadequate, we have it in the enormous labor annually entailed on the Legislature in trying to undo the mischiefs it has previously done.

— Attributed to Spencer's essay, "The Collective Wisdom."

No matter the wisdom of it, our unread politicians trumpet themselves into the legislative arena, anyway: badly advised, they eagerly jump in with their "legislative solutions," ones that invariably do not work, but which, ultimately, bring them and their laws into disrespect.

What the vote seeking politicians, and the social engineers from whom they take their advise, fail to understand, seemingly, is that there is a difference between that which is imaginable, and that which is probable. Nonetheless, on account of the seductive lure of socialism, philanthropic laws (general welfare by general plunder) do exist; but one cannot, at the same time, have philanthropic laws and just laws; one cannot, at the same time, be both a slave and a free man.

Passing laws in areas where laws should not be passed, considering the fundamental reason for the existence of laws, is a perversion. It brings on: first, disregard; then, contempt; and then, social disorder. At all points "it gives an exaggerated importance to political passions and conflicts, and to politics in general." (Bastiat.)

Legislation, The Suppressor of Truth:

Let us suppose I have yet to convince you, and you continue to be of the view that legislation can help us and make us, on the whole, better off. Let as further suppose that we have the scientific and technical know-how to put the whole thing together: then — is there still some problem? And, the answer is, yes — a very serious problem.

Legislation, by definition, is designed to throttle individual initiative and freedom. Wherever an individual suffers from a curtailment of his or her freedom, the untold suffering often will extend throughout the larger community in ways we are never quite able to comprehend. As science shows, it is the diversity of things, in the larger cosmos, which has led to the universe in which we now live; it is diversity in life which has brought to the universe the means by which it might comprehend itself, at its current level; it is the diversity in nature through which the human species evolved; it is diversity which maintains the species; and it is to diversity we must look if we think there is some improvement to be made. When a group of persons excessively denies diversity, that is to say denies freedom to the groups it wishes to suppress, then, in denying diversity, they deny the emergence of truth.

Whereas scientific and technological results are always due to relatively small minorities or particular individuals, often, if not always, in opposition to ignorant or indifferent majorities, legislation, especially today, always reflects the will of a contingent majority within a committee of legislators who are not necessarily more learned or enlightened than the dissenters. Where authorities and majorities prevail, as in legislation, individuals must yield, regardless of whether they are right or wrong.   — Leoni.

Legislation & The Rule of Law:

Common law, as we have seen, is law created and administered by the people: legislation is law created by the "majority" (read those in power) on the advice of "experts" at the expense of the "minority" (those out of power; or, those, for the time being, who do not care). Legislated law is like the old law of kings, the result of the sovereign 'majority' imposed upon the 'minority'; it inherently offends the rule of law.

The rule of law has a number of different meanings and corollaries. Its primary meaning is that everything must be done according to law. Applied to the powers of government, this requires that every government authority which does some act which would otherwise be a wrong (such as taking a man's land), or which infringes a man's liberty (as by refusing him planning permission), must be able to justify its action as authorized by law — and in nearly every case this will mean authorized by Act of Parliament. ... But the rule of law demands something more, since otherwise it would be satisfied by giving the government unrestricted discretionary powers, so that everything that they did was within the law. ... The secondary meaning of the rule of law, therefore, is that governments should be conducted within a framework of recognized rules and principles which restrict discretionary power. ... Thus the Home Secretary has a nominally unlimited power to revoke any television licence and a local planning authority may make planning permission subject to such conditions as it thinks fit, but the courts will not allow these powers to be used in ways which Parliament is not thought to have intended. ... Faced with the fact that Parliament freely confers discretionary powers with little regard to the dangers of abuse, the courts must attempt to strike a balance between the needs of fair and efficient administration and the need to protect the citizen against arbitrary government. ...

What the rule of law demands is not that wide discretionary power should be eliminated, but that the law should be able to control its exercise. ... The first requirement is the recognition that all power has legal limits. The next requirement, no less vital, is that the courts should draw those limits in a way which strikes the most suitable balance between executive efficiency and legal protection of the citizen. Parliament constantly confers upon public authorities powers which on their face might seem absolute and arbitrary. But arbitrary power and unfettered discretion are what the courts refuse to countenance. They have woven a network of restrictive principles which require statutory powers to be exercised reasonably and in good faith, for proper purposes only, and in accordance with the spirit as well as the letter of the empowering Act. They have also, as explained elsewhere, imposed stringent procedural requirements.
— Wade.

The discretion of a statutory body is never unfettered. It is a discretion which is to be exercised according to law. That means at least this: the statutory body must be guided by relevant considerations and not by irrelevant. If its decision is influenced by extraneous considerations which it ought not to have taken into account, then the decision cannot stand. No matter that the statutory body may have acted in good faith, nevertheless the decision will be set aside.
— Lord Denning, *Padfield v. Minister of Agriculture*, 1968, A.C

Positive Law:

... when the law, by means of its necessary agent, force, imposes upon men a regulation of labor, a method or a subject of education, a religious faith or creed — then the law is no longer negative; it acts positively upon people. It substitutes the will of the legislator for their own wills; the initiative of the legislator for their own initiatives. When this happens, the people no longer need to discuss, to compare, to plan ahead; [it being intended that] the law does all this for them. Intelligence becomes a useless prop for the people; they cease to be men; they lose their personality, their liberty, their property. — Bastiat.

It is not likely through any surveying techniques, now known, that any conclusions can be arrived at as to what people want for themselves. Even if we could list the wants and desires of mankind, the list would be as numerous and as diverse as the people themselves. The best one might expect from a survey is that there might be some agreement on a limited number of things as to what is *not* wanted. Professor Bruno Leoni:

The common will, conceived as the will common to each and every member of a society, is much more easily ascertainable, as far as its content is concerned, in the 'negative' way already evidenced by the Confucian principle than in any other 'positive' way. Nobody would contest the fact that an inquiry among any group whatsoever conducted with the object of ascertaining what its members do not want to suffer as a result of the direct action of other people on them would give clearer and more precise results than any inquiry relating to their wishes in other respects. Indeed, the celebrated rule of 'self-protection' propounded by John Stuart Mill not only can be reduced to the Confucian principle but becomes actually applicable only if so reduced, for nobody could effectively decide what is and what is not harmful to any particular individual in a given society without relying in the end upon the judgment of each member of that society. It is for all of them to define what is harmful, and this is, in fact, what any one of them would not want others to do to him.

In its barest form (and likely in the only workable form) laws are those which are restrictive and which relate to the collective organization of the individual's right to lawful defense. Restrictive law in not out to get anyone to do anything in particular; it is there to forbid something: criminal law is an example of restrictive law. Restrictive laws are employed to oblige the citizen to abstain from harming others. The preference for restrictive laws arises because any other approach will likely infringe a person's natural and prior existing rights.[5]

Legislation & Morals:

> Shame ... not fear, is the sheet-anchor of the law.
> — William Hazlitt.

There is a whole line of philosophical thought that has resulted in what has become known as the moral sentiment theory. It is a theory that asserts that the ethical system, on which society depends, is intuitive; people will generally do the right thing instinctively and not necessarily because of any understanding of the process, nor because they have reasoned things out in any particular manner.

There are those, Spooner having been among them, who believe that peace is an indispensable condition to a satisfactory life; this notion, they believe, and the obedience to it is the only universal obligation: everything else is a matter of personal choice. The canon by which these people live is to proceed at all times honestly; to hurt no one; and to give to every one his or her due.

Man, no doubt, owes many other moral duties to his fellow men; such as to feed the hungry, clothe the naked, shelter the homeless, care for the sick, protect the defenceless, assist the weak, and enlighten the ignorant. But these are simply moral duties, of which each man must be his own judge, in each particular case, as to whether, and how, and how far, he can, or will, perform them. But of his legal duty — that is, of his duty to live honestly towards his fellow men — his fellow men not only may judge, but, for their own protection, must judge.   — Spooner.

The argument is made that legislation is needed to infuse (as if it is possible) morals in the general population by the use of force (a self destructing argument). Leoni asserted that "legislation may have and actually has in many cases today a negative effect on the very efficacy of the rules and on the homogeneity of the feelings and convictions already prevailing in a given society. ... the very possibility of nullifying agreements and conventions through supervening legislation tends in the long run to induce people to fail to rely on any existing conventions or to keep any accepted agreements."

We need to look at the obverse of the proposition that legislation is needed because of the lack of morals, viz. that legislation is not generally needed on account of morals which naturally exist amongst the population. This is hardly a new thought. In international law we have the salutary but sanctionless code called the Comity of nations. The *OED* defines comity: "courtesy, civility, urbanity; kindly and considerate behavior towards others." Things generally do run, and will run very well, all things considered, simply due to the courteous and friendly understanding by which each of us proceeds to deal with his fellows. Persons, on the whole, proceed in a friendly way; because, on average, better results are obtained. The primary moral tenent is to treat another as the treater would like to be treated.[6]

Therefore, it is necessary for us to keep reminding ourselves, in respect to the various proceedings and usages in life, that each of us must proceed with the principal objective in life — the same for all of us, viz. to preserve our own rights and interests. This objective is best met by giving respect to others, in the same level and manner as the giver expects to receive in return.

Our legislatures have turned into mills, grinding out useless laws in most all areas. At all points, legislation gives an exaggerated importance to political passions and conflicts, and to politics in general. Certain kinds of legislation, inarguably, make things only more difficult for the very people we would like to help. This should be obvious to the average observer. But what is not so obvious are the problems brought on by such legislation which lie out of sight, and when, finally felt by the general population, cannot be cured without a heavy dose of time and pain. The underlying problem is this: passing laws in areas where laws should not be passed will first bring disregard, and then will come contempt for the law followed by social disorder. This process of disregard and contempt, while brought on by bad law, will take its toll on all laws, some of which are very important to the continued functioning of society.

The primitive individualism as described by Thomas Hobbes in 1660, is a myth. The savage is not solitary, and his instinct is collectivist. The rules of human conduct gradually evolved (particularly the rules governing the possession and exchange of property, viz. contract law). These rules were handed down by tradition, teaching and imitation, and consisted largely of prohibitions, that is to say law evolved to be restrictive in nature.

In conclusion, I quote Professor Bruno Leoni, yet once again (his work, *Freedom and the Law*, has proven to be such an inspiration):

Substituting legislation for the spontaneous application of non-legislated rules of behaviour is indefensible unless it is proved that the latter are uncertain or insufficient or that they generate some evil that legislation could avoid while maintaining the advantages of the previous system. This preliminary assessment is simply unthought of by contemporary legislators. On the contrary, they seem to think that legislation is always good in itself and that the burden of the proof is upon the people who do not agree. ...

These people pretend to champion democracy. But we ought always to remember that whenever majority rule is unnecessarily substituted for individual choice, democracy is in conflict with individual freedom. It is this particular kind of democracy that ought to be kept to a minimum in order to preserve a maximum of democracy compatible with individual freedom. ...

Legislation, especially if applied to the innumerable choices that individuals make in their daily life, appears to be something absolutely exceptional and even contrary to the rest of what takes place in human society. The most striking contrast between legislation and other processes of human activity emerges whenever we compare the former with the proceedings of science. I would even say that this is one of the greatest paradoxes of contemporary civilization: it has developed scientific methods to such an astonishing degree while at the same time extending, adding, and fostering such antithetic procedures as those of decision groups and majority rule.

I leave off with a reference to Shakespeare, who set forth a compendium of the law in his works. If the law appeals to one as a study, it's not likely because of the characters that flood the history of law, as interesting as they may be. Rather its appeal, like that of all art, "lies in the variety of its inherent antitheses — the opposition of Is and Ought, of positive and natural law, legitimate and revolutionary law, freedom and order, justice and equity, law and mercy." (Phillips.)

_____

"On Property Rights."

> ... Man is not like the brutes, limited to the present time, either in enjoyment or suffering; but that he is susceptible of pleasure and pain by anticipation — Bentham.

> The power of perpetuating our property in our families is one of the most valuable and interesting circumstances belonging to it, and that which tends the most to the perpetuation of society itself. It makes our weakness subservient to our virtue; it grafts benevolence even upon avarice. — Burke.

Real and Personal Property:

William Graham Sumner[1] described property as a "most fundamental and complex of social facts." Given Sumner's description, it will be no surprise to learn that the legal rules surrounding the possession and transfer of property are equally "fundamental and complex." I make no attempt to sort out these rules or to explain their complexities, here, at this place. But, I choose to say this much: property, as most do understand, is something physical, something that can be possessed. Lawyers break it down into two categories real property (land) and personal property (moveable stuff).[2] Personal property, for the purposes of discussion, can be further broken down, physically speaking, into two sub-categories: into that which is easily possessed (pocket property) and that which is not so easily possessed (jumbo property). "Jumbo property" and real property are by their nature difficult or impossible to be physically possessed by a person or a group of persons; guardians are often employed to watch over these kinds of property. With personal property, possession is often good enough to show ownership. Not so with the other kinds of property. Because it cannot be physically possessed there is often difficulty in proving ownership; invariably, papers will have to be produced. (As a lawyer, I can tell you that much paper comes about when ever the question of ownership comes into play in respect to real property and/or "jumbo property.") Now, it is much easier to move paper around than the property itself (indeed, real property, by its nature, cannot be moved at all). In the final analysis, it's not the paper that is of value. The paper (more and more, now, it's just so much electronic bits and bites) is but a large social accounting system to keep track of who owns what.

The Three Great Principles of English Law:

The right to possess and use property is a legal concept. It is a right which can only be lawfully obtained through the creation of the property itself, or more commonly in advanced societies, through a voluntary exchange between people by way of contract — "I will trade you this right of mine, in exchange for that right of yours." The beauty of a contract is that it comes about on a strictly voluntary basis, with the state only getting involved to enforce the contractual obligations where they are not voluntarily discharged by the parties themselves: and, which they do, 99.9% of the time. Without the legal concept of contract nothing would move in our economy and we all would have to go back to the caves. Thus, it is, that property and the full freedom to deal with it has become essential to civilization.[3] The right to our property and the right to do with it as we wish, within the bounds of criminal law, is something to be left entirely to the citizens. This is and has been the great canon which has guided people into civilized society. It is one of the three great principles of English law as was stated by Blackstone. First is the Security of the Person. Second is the Liberty of the Person. And Third, "inherent in every Englishman," the Right to Hold Property.[4] Though, as you will see from the arguments next following, the possession of property is a natural right — the reason the right to hold property is one of three great principles of English law (indeed, I would assert, the great principle upon which the others rest) is, that, as a practical matter, if a person, who labors to bring property into existence or into a useful form, believes that he might lose it to the first brute who comes along — why, then, that person will not make the effort in the first place. The end result will be that the life sustaining products, meant for the consumption of all, will, therefore, not come into existence, and; well — without basic security, food and shelter; it is useless to talk of the value of life and liberty. Only when a nation is wealthy, will the great numbers of people of which it is composed have the basics with which to carry on in life. "The natural tenancy," as Macaulay has said, "Of every society in which property enjoys tolerable security is to increase wealth." That wealth is created by different people in different degrees depending on their natural talents and greater opportunities, is beside the point.[5]

Possession of Property as a Natural Right:

Is the recognition of the right to possess property, natural, or not? Or, is it just a creature of the law? To answer these questions will take some acquaintance with the political thoughts as expressed by Thomas Hobbes and John Locke, and more generally, on one's view of the nature of man.[6]

That people have a right to possess all the property which have come into their hands as the fruit of their labor or through voluntary trade, is, I submit, a natural right.[7] This proposition raises the question as to what life was like to pre-civil man. We first turn to Hobbes.

Hobbesian Theory:

Thomas Hobbes wrote a book, which he called the *Leviathan*, a treatise on the origin and ends of government. While I deal with Hobbes and his work elsewhere, I am obliged to say a few words at this place. *Leviathan* was written during the time of the Puritan Commonwealth, and was a defence to "secular monarchy." To Hobbes "Good" and "evil" are inconsistent names applied haphazardly by different people depending on what might attract or repel them. This egotistical psychology, according to the theory, made the life of man in a pre-social state of nature, "nasty, brutish and short, a constant war of everyman with everyman." Hobbes then draws an inference or comes to a conclusion which does not follow from the premise: *non sequitur*. Somehow, man — nasty, brutish and unrational, as Hobbes thought he might have been — became rational and enlightened, such that he put himself under government. Thus, for our purposes here, it is important to understand Hobbes' view that the first principle of human behavior was egoism, or self-interest; and it was this egoism, that was the root of all social conflict. Hobbes had a nauseating view of man in his natural state (a state which, I should mention in passing, lasted millions of years); men were no better, seemingly worse, than a bunch of animals.

Lockian Theory:

John Locke, while likewise justifying the existence of government, had different views than that of Hobbes. Locke, consistent with his philosophy, viewed man as naturally moral.[8] The reason man would willingly contract into civil society is not to shake off his supposed brutish state, but rather that he may advance his ends (peace and security) in a more efficient manner. To achieve his ends, man gives up, in favor of the state, a certain amount of his personal power and freedom. Locke maintained that the original state of nature was happy and characterized by reason and tolerance. He further maintained that all human beings, in their natural state, were equal and free to pursue life, health, liberty, and possessions; and that these were inalienable rights.[9] Pre-social man, as a moral being and as an individual, contracted out "into civil society by surrendering personal power to the ruler and magistrates," and did so as "a method of securing natural morality more efficiently." To Locke, natural justice exists and this is so whether the state exists, or not, it is just that the state might better guard natural justice.

Locke taught that individual property, along with life and liberty, was a natural right — a right existing in the state of nature.[10] The only purpose of government, according to Locke, is the preservation of these pre-existing natural rights. It follows, incidentally, that since the ownership of property is a natural right, the state, in the taking of it through taxation, save the situation where the individual consents, does so by breaching one of the three fundamental rights: the right to life, the right to liberty, and the right to property.

Labor Theory of Value:

One prominent theory of value is grounded on the notion that the origin of property is labor. Labor — the "exertion of the faculties of the body or mind" — is, indeed, indispensable to the production of most property.[11] Whether the resulting product, or commodity of production, has value, or not, may have little to do with the labor spent in bringing it into being. Value is "that amount of some commodity, medium of exchange, ... which is considered to be an equivalent for something else; a fair or adequate equivalent or return." Value is not determined by the maker or makers of the commodity; it is determined by the market.

Thomas Carlyle, an individual who had much influence during the 19th century, preached that "work is noble." To Carlyle, as was the case for Marx who came after him, labor was the real source of wealth. John Stuart Mill spread the same idea in his work, *Principles of Political Economy* (1848), where he concluded that the production of wealth came about only through physical human activity. Mill concluded — wrongly, as so many economists have done since — that a value, as struck by the market of any particular commodity or service, is the result of some person's or persons' labor, and not (which in fact it is) a signal to a person or persons that they have made a right (or for that matter a wrong) decision or series of decisions, encouraging others to do, or not to do likewise. Value and labor cannot be equated.

So the thought is, that a man gains a right to property because he removed something from nature and mixed his labor with it. And this is so, as long as he keeps possession of it. A right to property, by long established law, comes from the possession of it.[12] Of course, he may be deprived of his possession of it, if it can be proven that he took possession of it illegally through fraud or thief,[13] otherwise he has a right to it whether he took a hand in the production of it, or not. This is a very important point which was lost on many early economists. Belief that property rights were founded in labor (Labor Theory of Value) is wrong and has led to some fruitless economic conjectures. Worse, such a theory in the heads of collectivists proved to be, as history will readily show, destructive to the state and the overall welfare of mankind.

A Side Note on Inheritance:

Locke's theory of property, while primarily resting on the right of labor to what it produced and on the ability of man to acquire it through legitimate trading activities, allows that a person might acquire property through inheritance. This question of inheritance is one that has long bothered me as it did Blackstone:

> Pleased as we are with the possession, we seem afraid to look back to the means by which it was acquired, as if fearful of some defect in our title... not caring to reflect that (accurately and strictly speaking) there is no foundation in nature or in natural law, why a set of words upon parchment should convey the domination of land: why the son should have a right to exclude his fellow-creatures from a determinate spot of ground, because his father had done so before him: or why the occupier of a particular field or of a jewel, when lying on his death-bed, and no longer able to maintain possession, should be entitled to tell the rest of the world which of them should enjoy it after him.

But, really, inheritance is something that should no more bother us than that which is inherent in the nature of ownership: the right to give a gift of your property to another. Or, for that matter to lend one's property to another, for a price (whether it be a fixed rate [interest] or for a piece of the action [profit]). Thus arose a system of capital which went beyond the labor theory of value, and which Marx condemned as exploitation.

A Constitutional Right, The Right to Property:

The *raison d'être* of government — and, this is classic (Locke *et al.*) — is for the protection of property rights. It follows, therefore, in order to legitimize government, that property rights must be incorporated as a cornerstone to a country's constitution.[14] As a practical matter, such a preservation is essential. Let me make just two arguments.

The first argument: A country's economy is driven by the enterprise of its citizens; one could call it "free enterprise," but for myself, I would call it "independent enterprise," that is — free enterprise under the rule of law. There is, as is to be taken from the lessons of history, no other production and distribution system to which a freedom loving population can turn — absolutely, none.

The second argument, which is simply a repetition of the Lockeian theory previously set out, depends on an understanding of each of the concepts of both property and government, and the interrelationship of these two concepts. What is property? Property is a thing, short of another person, which, within the bounds of natural law, a person can use. Property comes about through the productiveness and inventiveness of a person or persons.

Governments, essential to larger societal groups, came into being at the very earliest part of human history. All any of us can do is to speculate; but many, many, years must have passed before humans went about organizing themselves beyond a simple family group, or a tribe. For the well-being of any group — or, for that matter, an individual — the exercise of discipline and control is always necessary. It is important to accept, in these developments, that people in their primitive state (before governments came into existence) recognized the concept of personal property, being the right to possess and call certain property their own. As a corollary right, there is the right to defend (either themselves personally or through the agency of another, or others) against any person or group who is about to deprive them of their property. The important point, however, in this analysis, is that, on the time continuum, the notion of property precedes the notion of government. There exists, in connection with society's political organization, an unspoken compact between all the members of society, that governments are necessary and therefore formed "for the mutual preservation of their lives, liberties, and estates, which I call by the general name, property." (Locke, 1690.)

A Note on Enterprise and Money:

On looking up the definition of the word enterprise one should find this, "the readiness to engage in undertakings, to obligate oneself to do something." Enterprise, is to the right of ownership, as a house is to its foundation. Enterprise is dependant on the right of ownership. Except in certain private relationships, it is in the nature of an enterprise for a person to give over his or her labor, or the fruits thereof, in exchange for the labor, or the fruits of labor, of another. The fruits of labor are objects which, if desired by a significant number of other humans, may be valuable in exchange for other objects or goods. In our system of free exchange it is goods which we exchange; more often than not, in our modern society, goods will be found only on one side of the exchange, on the other side will be found money. Money is a voucher which the population readily recognizes as an answerable call on goods in the system, now or in the future. While money is not the only voucher acting as evidence of transferable rights of ownership, it is, by far and away, in a stable system, the most readily recognizable, the most acceptable and the most transferable. Things do not work well without money; without money one is left with a very primitive and unwieldy system of barter. Money is property rights. Money only works well as a medium of exchange when people have an absolute faith in it as a way to store, even for a small amount of time, the fruits of labor. Without faith in their country's money, people will be inexorably drawn first to a barter system, and its inefficiencies; then to anarchy and revolution and the human misery attending. Thus, property rights are essential to the constitution of a country.

Slave State:

When one imagines a state vested with all property rights (read the power of confiscation) and the individual with none, then one imagines the desperate state or life of the slave; it is exactly the same feeling which a member has in a collectivist setup. In an absolute state of slavery everything belongs to the master or masters. A slave is powerless and senses it; he or she has no self-esteem or ambition: and this because, by the very definition of slavery, the individual is reduced to having no property rights. A collectivist state is a state of many slaves and a few masters (as such it can never last long). The notions of property rights and slavery are inextricably tied up with one another. It follows, therefore — if freedom, or liberty is the highest good — that property is to belong to those, without infringing the rights of another, who acquire it.

Achilles' Heel — Lack Of Husbandry:

No one has to be told about how pride of ownership will normally compel a person to take care of what he or she owns. It applies to items of personal use. Importantly, it also applies to all capital goods in this vast economy of ours.

Arthur Seldon:

The central advantage of capitalism over socialism in the husbandry of property is that the real owners in capitalism take care of their property; the nominal owners in socialism cannot because they do not know what they own. What belongs nominally to every one on paper belongs in effect to no-one in practice. Coalfields, railways, schools and hospitals that are owned 'by the people' are in real life owned by phantoms. No nominal owner can sell, hire, lend, bequeath or give them to family, friends or good causes. Public ownership is a myth and a mirage. It is the false promise and the Achilles' heel of socialism.

The effort required to 'care' for the 50-millionth individual share of a hospital or school owned by 50 million people, even if identifiable, would far outweigh the benefit; so it is not made, even if it could be. The task is deputed to public servants answerable to politicians who in turn are in socialist mythology answerable to the people. In this long line of communication the citizen is often in effect disenfranchised. The wonder is that the myth of public ownership continues to be propagated by men and women who aspire to political leadership.

If one owns assets then they will see to the careful management and employment of them. No one has to tell owners of property the importance of this; no one has to pass out rewards for the proper use of an asset, or exact punishment for improper use. The advantage of ownership is gained in its proper use of it: lost in its improper use. When an owner misuses his property and he devalues it or loses it; he has no one to blame but himself. When an owner puts his property to good use and experiences a gain thereby; then, likewise, he can thank himself. No third party need be thanked or blamed. Harmony comes about naturally when people have ownership in the assets that they use or employ.

"On Rights."

When the question comes to mind, What rights do we have? There should come to mind the figure, as tradition has it, of a veiled woman who declares, "My name is Duty, turn and follow me."[1]

I write here not so much of those rights which accrue to those who operate under society's rules, the rights to which Edmund Burke referred when he wrote:

If civil society be made for the advantage of man, all the advantages for which it is made become his right. It is an institution of beneficence; and law itself is only beneficence acting by a rule. Men have a right to live by that rule; they have a right to do justice, as between their fellows, whether their fellows are in public function or in ordinary occupation. They have a right to the fruits of their industry ... Whatever each man can separately do, without trespassing upon others, he has a right to do for himself; and he has a right to a fair portion of all which society, with all its combinations of skill and force, can do in his favor. In this partnership all men have equal rights, but not to equal things.
— *Reflections On The Revolution In France.*

I write, as Jefferson did, of "inalienable rights," rights which accrue to human existence.[2] I have written elsewhere "On Liberty" and "On Property Rights" — I do not intend to go over that territory again, other than to state this: the right to liberty and the right to possess property are the most important in our hierarchy of fundamental rights.

Fundamental or constitutional rights, as I emphasized in my treatment of the rights to liberty and to property, are not simply just nice things for you and me and other individuals to have; they are fundamental to the existence of harmony and prosperity of the whole of society.[3] If fundamental rights are encroached upon to any significant degree — and this is in their nature — a peaceful social structure in which we would all like to operate will collapse. In the wake of such a collapse, many will suffer deprivation, misery and death. These rights are "inalienable," or as the French in 1789 defined them, "natural and imprescriptible," because they are essential to people as they go about caring for themselves and their family. This is particularly so of the right to be free. In many parts of this world man still wears the shackles of others. This is so even within the most advanced societies, such as we might claim exists in the United States and in Canada. No matter that we may think we have come a long way from feudal times when the only rights that existed were those as were possessed by the Lord of the Manor, it can be a short route back. Though the players will be wearing different masks, we are never that far away from dark times.[4]

> Unlike in appearance and names as it may be to the old order of slaves and serfs, working under masters, who were coerced by barons, who were themselves vassals of dukes or kings, the new order wished for, constituted by workers under foremen of small groups, overlooked by superintendents, who are subject to higher local managers, who are controlled by superiors of districts, themselves under a central government, must be essentially the same in principle. In the one case, as in the other, there must be established grades, and enforced subordination of each grade to the grades above. This is a truth which the communist or the socialist does not dwell upon.   — Spencer, "A Plea for Liberty."

Constitutional history is a subject I treat elsewhere. Sufficient to say here, Canada's constitution took on its own identity with the *The British North America Act* — the first recital of which expressed the desire of the people to be federally united "with a constitution similar in Principle to that of the United Kingdom." We had, in 1867, simply adopted the civil rights for which England was and is known. Rights which Canadians, because of their British ancestry, have recognized as their own since before confederation. These rights came about only through deep and long struggles culminating in historical declarations, such as: the *Magna Carta*[5] of 1215, the *Petition of Right*[6] of 1628, and the *English Bill of Rights*[7] of 1689.

It is with these declarations, and more importantly, with the development of the English common law, that Englishmen did and do lay claim to rights, the inherent rights of a free people. It was never thought necessary to write these rights down on a piece of paper. Great Britain has not written up their fundamental rights in a written constitution as we have done in Canada and as the United States did long ago? Why should it be done? The classic response was that as was given by James Madison: civil rights must be entrenched in a country's constitution, there, to be an "impenetrable bulwark against every assumption of power in the legislative or executive." Let me emphasize: the listing of these fundamental rights in a written constitution, by that act, does not create these rights. All of these rights were possessed by British citizens before the American Revolution of 1776. Under the English common law — and this is the basis for its strength and longevity — we start out as a full vessel, as John Locke described; and not empty as Thomas Hobbes thought. We are, to begin with, independent and free. Government being but a construct cannot give us a thing, and it certainly cannot give us rights. "Constitutional rights," cannot be created by a country's constitution, though they may well be affirmed in writing by it. The reason for this and the reason for the irrefragable nature of such rights, is that to be human is to have such rights: these rights, these basic human rights existed way before any one dreamt up the idea of writing up a constitution.

Since 1982, Canadians need but look to *The Charter* to see that they have the right to freedom of conscience, religion, thought, belief, opinion and expression; and freedom of peaceful assembly. (Section 2.) In respect to the rights of the citizen in his or her dealings with government, he or she is to be "secure against unreasonable search or seizure," (section 8) "not to be arbitrarily detained or imprisoned," (section 9) to be allowed to "retain and instruct counsel without delay and to be informed of that right," (section 10) to be "informed without unreasonable delay of the specific offence," with which he or she may be charged, to be "tried within a reasonable time," "not to be compelled to be a witness in proceedings against that person in respect of the offence," and to be "presumed innocent until proven guilty according to law in a fair and public hearing by an independent and impartial tribunal." (These last few to be found in section 11.)[8]

So, our constitutional rights, whether written or not, are to be an "impenetrable bulwark" against the power of government. If, however, government does trench upon our fundamental rights — what recourse is there for the citizen? Here is a quote from an old English decision:

> If the plaintiff has a right, he must of necessity have a means to vindicate and maintain it; and, indeed, it is a vain thing to imagine a right without a remedy; for want of right and want of remedy are reciprocal. It is no objection to say that it will occasion multiplicity of actions; for if men will multiply injuries, actions must be multiplied too; for every man that is injured ought to have his recompense.
> — Lord Holt, *Ashby v. Aylesbury*, 1702.

Here in Canada, *The Charter* of 1982, notwithstanding its serious flaws, has given a clearly visible platform upon which our judges might take a stand against big government. I have gained the impression that the courts, in spite of great pressures, have by and large taken a conservative approach. Our judges are aware of the great common law principles which underlie our constitution. It is comforting to know that such a body as our judiciary exists; the typical politician is ill-equipped and ill-motivated in coming to grips with the most delicate task of reconciling liberty and order. To the extent we place ourselves under government, we lose, we hope only to the least degree, our freedom. The trade is liberty versus order, individual freedom versus majority rule, the rights of the majority versus the rights of the various minorities; these trades must always be kept in proper balance and cool judicial minds need to do the monitoring.

———————————

"Criminal Law & Drugs."

These records of wars, intrigues, factions, and revolutions, are so many collections of experiments, by which the politician or moral philosopher fixes the principles of his science, in the same manner as the physician or natural philosopher becomes acquainted with the nature of plants, minerals, and other external objects, by the experiments which he forms concerning them.[1]   — David Hume.

Our long armed and hairy ancestors had no idea of redress beyond vengeance, or of justice beyond mere individual reprisal.   — John Marshall Gest.

To determine what constitutes criminal law is, as one learned judge has opined, "a work of art, it is something that may be easier to recognize than define ..."[2] I venture to say that when a person commits a crime that person commits a breach of faith with the community in which that person lives. In such an event the community, as a collective whole, in a self-protective act, will assert itself against the criminal. Criminal law is a method of enabling men to live together in a community in spite of the possibility that their desires may conflict. Historically, punishment has been the manner by which the community attempts to deter crime,[3] and generally the criminal offense has been, throughout history, gauged and matched to a suitable punishment. As to what individual acts the community has considered to be crimes and as to what punishment it has meted out, makes for an interesting historical study, which I do not now have the time to carry out.[4]

Of course, it is no longer the sovereign who defines crime, that is now the function of our democratically elected assemblies. However, such an assembly cannot make an act into a crime, as our Supreme Court here in Canada has stated, unless "we can properly look for some evil or injurious or undesirable effect upon the public against which the law is directed. That effect may be in relation to social, economic or political interests; and the legislature has had in mind to suppress the evil or to safeguard the interest threatened."[5]

Further, it can be "neither a static catalogue of offences nor order of sanctions. The evolving and transforming types and patterns of social and economic activities are constantly calling for new penal controls and limitations and that new modes of enforcement and punishment adapted to the changing conditions are not to be taken as being equally within the ambit of parliamentary power is, in my opinion, not seriously arguable."[6]

In the case of *RJR - Macdonald v. Canada* (1995), the Supreme Court of Canada determined that the exercise of the power to make an act a criminal one, a test is to be applied; one "of substance, not form." To be fully fledged criminal law, the act prohibited "must pose a significant, grave and serious risk of harm to public health, morality, safety or security ..."

And so how does this established judicial view apply to the business of keeping in check those substances which may prove to be harmful to the individuals who misuse them?

As to the nature of the various illegitimate drugs and their effect on human beings — well, I shall have to leave that to the medical doctors, but I just simply wonder, what is so wrong with drugs that we as a country should have to spend so much money on fighting (maybe this should read encouraging) the distribution and use of drugs? Oliver Wendell Holmes wondered, too! "That all spasmodic cerebral action is an evil is not perfectly clear. Men get fairly intoxicated with music, with poetry, with religious excitement — oftenest with love. ... There are forms and stages of alcoholic exaltation which, in themselves, and without regard to their consequences, might be considered as positive improvements of the persons affected."

To borrow the words of Edmund Burke: "It looks to me to be narrow and pedantic, to apply the ordinary ideas of criminal justice to this great public contest." Endless drug wars will never make drug prohibition work, even if the drug fighters turn our country into a police state. Indeed, the dynamics of law enforcement and drug markets guarantee that drug prohibition will always backfire, tragically.[7] Since law enforcement resources are limited, pursuing more drug offenders means fewer officers available to pursue non-drug offenders, such as muggers, arsonists, burglars, robbers and rapists. It is to be remembered in all of this that the acquisition and use of drugs are usually non-violent activities. In the United States, 76% of the those imprisoned have no violent crime record. We can only presume that those serving time for selling drugs constitute a great part of these non-violent cases. In recent years there has been a flood of drug cases. This flood is contributing to the collapse of our criminal justice system; our court dockets and our prisons are crowded bringing forth conditions which are hardly conducive to the delivery of justice. The principal trouble with anti-drug laws is the same trouble as can be found with all laws: as Jeremy Bentham said, years ago,

"Every law is an infraction of liberty." And the liberty of her citizens — as defined by John Stuart Mill as being "that of pursuing our own good in our own way, so long as we do not attempt to deprive others of theirs, or impede their efforts to obtain it" — is the essential foundation upon which Canada is built; no hammers can be allowed to strike at this foundation unless for very good reason.

What, specifically, are the arguments for drug laws? First off — we have to prevent people from harming themselves. So, putting them in jail is preventing them from harming themselves! Should we pass laws that might "help" troubled anorectics and bulimics in our society. Should we make the owners and managers of food supermarkets criminals. One simply has to question why we place the blame for destructive drug habits on the people who sell drugs. Well, how about: to prevent people from committing crime. Our existing approach has been to create crimes were there were none before, and to entrap people into a life of crime, a course they would likely not have followed if the taking of drugs was, in the first place, a legal activity.

Another argument: drug use hurts family and friends. I am sure in some situations this is perfectly true, so, is this a good reason to pass a criminal law against it? If so, then how about jail terms for those who practise other hurtful behavior towards friends and family?

The fourth argument: there are economic conse-quences to drug use. Well, like a lot of human activities — yes, drugs can impact on the economic abilities of those who become involved with them; an individual may just "drug out" all day long and not get down to doing any work. One must question the premise upon which such an argument is founded. Is it not repulsive to reduce the measure of human worth to a person's productive capacity. At any rate, there is much 'unproductive' behavior of people in our society, and drug use is likely one of them; but we should not — as I suspect we have with this drug law question — take an "effect" and label it a "cause."

The conclusion to be reached — and this assumes one has some familiarity with what is going on in our streets and courts today — is that anti-drug laws not only do not help at getting at the real cause of what drives people to abuse themselves with poisonous substances; but that anti-drug laws exacerbate the problem. Never mind that our government is spending our scarce resources on an unwinnable war with drugs — anti-drug laws create crime and corruption; they prevent sensible medical use of certain of these drugs; and (this could be the most serious problem of anti-drug laws) they promote state activity that infringes on our constitutional rights of liberty and privacy. In the final analysis, it must be understood, that no man-made law can do away with the existence of drugs, and that, notwithstanding what the law says, or does not say about the subject — with the existence of drugs comes the existence of drug abusers. Criminal law will not limit drug abuse; it will, as our experience will now show, increase it. The only way to deal with the evil of drug abuse is the same way we deal with any moral evil: acknowledge its existence, debate it, and discredit it. Or more precisely — education, not criminal law, is the answer.

_____

"Crime & Punishment."

The first intent of laws Was to correct the effect, and check the cause, And all the ends of punishment Were only future mischiefs to prevent.[1]

Criminal Justice:

The first question is, What is a crime? It is an act injurious to another person, or group of persons. Not all injurious acts are crimes. It is a crime only when the offense is of such a grave character that its occurrence would likely cause, in the "average citizen," a horror or an extreme repugnance or disgust. But, more than that, I suggest — a crime is an act, which, while it might be injurious to a particular person (though not necessarily[2]), is injurious to the body politic.[3] As a practical matter, though while there are presumably constitutional limits, a crime is any act which the legislative assembly has defined as being a crime.[4] Further, as a practical distinction, a person who has allegedly committed a crime is pursued and prosecuted by the state. A crime is to be compared to an act injurious to another person and which has not been defined as a crime. An example is the breaching of a legal contract. Another example is where one acts carelessly, though unintentionally, so as to cause damage or injury to another (negligence). In these cases the offending person maybe pursued in a court of law, at the discretion of the injured party. This is called a civil suit, which is to be compared to a criminal prosecution.

It is to be remembered, under our system of government, that each of us has surrendered up to the state our natural right to revenge ourselves or our families for wrongs done. Punishment, because of our "social contract," might only be meted out by the state and only then after a formal proceeding conducted with due regard to constitutional safeguards. We have become especially sensitive to the state and its processes in respect to punishing a citizen. This sensitivity is traceable back to the times of the Star Chamber.[5] The fact of the matter is that the criminal law, in years past and yet today in parts of the world, has been used as an efficient engine for the purposes of political and religious prosecution. I quote Roscoe Pound:

> It is an inherent difficulty in the administration of punitive justice that criminal law has a much closer connection with politics than has the law of civil relations. There is no great danger of oppression through civil litigation. There is constant fear of oppression through the criminal law. Not only is one class suspicious of attempts by another to force its ideas upon the community under penalty of prosecution, but the power of a majority to visit with punishment practices which a strong minority consider in no way objectionable is liable to abuse and, whether rightly or wrongly used, puts a strain upon criminal law and administration.

Punishment:

First we define the crime, then we keep watch. Where we detect a crime and come up with a suspect, we charge the suspect. All necessary processes, but ones which must be done under our constitutional laws.[6] Once the state, through its police, on reasonable grounds, believes a person has committed a crime then the suspected criminal is brought to account. The prosecution of an alleged criminal, in our justice system, is an elaborate process. At the end of the process, we then might be in a position to declare the person to be guilty of the crime and thus to be a convicted criminal. What then is next? What is it that we are to do with convicted criminals?

Well, traditionally, we punish them, and we do so, for good reasons, reasons such as deterrence and retribution. We may, quite aside from punishment, try to rehabilitate convicted criminals so that they will become law abiding citizens. Or, as seems to be the case these days punish and attempt to rehabilitate all at the same time.

More generally, punishment is one of the pillars of justice; it is to be meted out mercifully in a measure suited to the crime. "The only true way to make the mass of mankind see the beauty of justice is by showing to them in pretty plain terms the consequences of injustice." (Sydney Smith.) With law comes the notion, according to John Locke, of either reward or punishment.[7]

Retribution:

It is to be remembered that one of the primary reasons for the law's existence, indeed the state's existence, is that people are to be relieved of their need to strike out against those who have wronged them. Not to argue the rights or wrongs of it, it is entirely natural for an individual, when injured or harmed by another or others, to seek revenge and retribution. It is potentially harmful to the state if it does not satisfy these needs, these urges. If the people are not satisfied, as history clearly shows, then the people take the law into their own hands, and they will do so, quick enough, if they see that the law does not suit their purposes. To punish the criminal, in order to satisfy the urges of the victim for revenge and retribution is an expression of a very old law, which still finds expression in our existing law, *lex talionis*[8]. *The Mosaic Code* of "an eye for an eye and a tooth for a tooth" lurks behind most legal punishments.

Deterrence:

People are driven to do, or not to do things, by the twin engines of hope and fear. Apprehension or dread of something that will or may happen in the future: it is this simple reaction to the promise of punishment which harnesses most and keeps them straight on the road of law and order.[9] We aim to deter future wrongdoers by punishing past offenders. Where deterrence is the only purpose, then, that punishment is to be preferred which combines the greatest deterrence with the least pain. For those who possess property then the taking away of their property by the levying of a fine maybe a sufficient deterrence. But fines hardly work against those who have nothing to lose. What is left is either imprisonment or the threat of corporal punishment. However, as Mencken was to observe, the choice of imprisonment or fine, is a choice of "allowing one prisoner to pay a bribe for his liberty, and taking away the liberty of another prisoner because he hasn't got the bribe."

Removement:

The removal of the convicted criminal may be solely motivated by the desire of making sure that the person no longer has the opportunity to commit crime. One might well be of the view that a convicted criminal is "social garbage" to be dealt with accordingly. Put them in prison and keep them there. A less expensive way of removement, though certainly drastic, is to put them to death. Removement is a justification for capital punishment, though probably the deterrence factor is more prominent. If dead, a convicted criminal cannot commit more crimes. Imprisonment is a more, very much more, expensive way of removement. A whole attitude in regards capital punishment and prisons might well be summed up in the view expressed by Thomas Huxley, we should keep criminals only if we believe, with some certainty, that they may become "serviceable members of the polity."

Rehabilitation:

A view, prevalent to the late 20th century, is that a person who commits a crime suffers from a disease. Thus, "humanitarians," applying Freudian principles, caring less for victims or the general peaceful state of society — apologize and excuse the criminal. It seems the vast majority of criminals are inflicted with a neurosis, or whatever, and they neither can help themselves in respect to its onset or its cure. What we need to do, is to help these people, not punish them. "The idea seems to be," as H.L. Mencken wrote, "to turn the dungeons and bullpens of the law into laboratories of the uplift, so that the man who goes in a burglar will come out a Y.M.C.A. secretary." The result of these "humanitarian views," is, that we send criminals off to institutions which are hardly prisons, at least as we have imagined them to be. One has to wonder. Oh, Sure! They are restricted, but prisoners, it seems to me, are sent to places which are more like retreats. These places have the accoutrements of a country club. There, the prisoner has immediately available to him services not generally available to a lot of law abiding citizens. This generous service is delivered through the agency of our government by the rest of us; we, who often cannot find the time to get a game of golf in or get off to the gym because we are too busy working for a living. In any event, is it that we can change a criminal, a person who in his pursuit of life is deliberate, habitual and incurable in his acts to advance himself at the expense of others. For most, I believe there is no cure. The rest of us who proceed in life serving others in exchange for a living, must but take steps to protect ourselves from such individuals. As Mencken points out, the vast majority of these people don't mind going to prison, especially the prisons of today; why, to "be bagged now and then, to make occasional sojourns in prison — all that, to him, is mere professional risk. When, by some mischance, he is taken and jailed, he lays the business to the fortunes of war ..."

What's To Be Done?

Here, in Canada, we can trace our existing criminal code to that which was passed in 1892. Though there has been some attempt to restructure and to check its growth and to make it logically consistent,[10] the Criminal Code of Canada is the same beast that came into being over a hundred years ago, and, since, has grown even more into an agglomeration of forbidden acts and transactions as has been dreamt up by successive political conclaves. It is, without a doubt a hodge-podge, a farrago, an unmethodical assemblage, a galimatias. It is full of repeating and disjointed sections most all of it written in arcane language which confuses and confounds the most experienced magistrates. The average officer of the law can not work with it. And as for the chances of the citizenry, whom the code is meant to govern, coming to an understanding of what acts are criminal and what are not; well — forget it: there is absolutely no chance. A citizen — outside of the acts of murder, assault, robbery and alike — will only know he has run afoul the criminal law when a policeman has come to his door to advise him of such. The Criminal Code, from start to finish needs to be rewritten, so to simplify and reduce.[11]

"The more laws there are the more crimes there will be", said the founder of Taoism about the sixth century B.C. As the Lord Chancellor in a recent speech well said — "The respect which the people of this country show to law and order is our greatest guarantee of getting through difficult times and it is incumbent upon the legislator to remember that when he piles one law upon another he may endanger that respect." So it may be the task of future reformers of the law to agitate for the elimination from our criminal code of many of the innumerable offences which involve only what Dr. Radzinowicz terms "administrative criminality" and evoke no moral reprobation except in so far as any breach of the existing law is reprehensible.[12]

Once a person is found through a fail safe process to be a criminal, then, he ought to be punished, taking into account the factors considered: retribution, deterrence and rehabilitation. The process ought to take in account the wishes of the victim and/or his family, and, if so willing, they should be brought right in on the process. It maybe that the determination of the appropriate sentence, ought, in the first instance, be left to a specialized group. Benjamin Cardozo:

Among students of criminology there are now many who maintain that the whole business of sentencing criminals should be taken away from the judges and given over to the doctors. Courts, with their judges and juries, are to find the fact of guilt or innocence. The fact being ascertained, the physician is to take the prisoner in hand and say what shall be done with him. ... after guilt has been determined by legal process, instead of sentence being fixed by judges according to statute, I should like to see offenders who have been adjudged guilty detained by the state. They should then be carefully studied by a board of expert mental and physical specialists, who after careful study of all the elements entering each case would decide and fix the penalty for the crime. I realize the complexity of such a fundamental change. It probably even requires a constitutional amendment.

A factor which should weigh in large is whether a respected member of the community might come forward, hopefully one from the criminal's own family. Where no such person is willing to come forward, then the criminal is to be left to face the severest of penalties.[13] Now, a person who undertakes some specific responsibility on behalf of another who remains primarily liable, or who makes himself liable for the default or miscarriage of another, or for the performance of some act on his part, is a person who is going to have to make a very careful assessment of the individual for whom he vouches. Why should a person put his reputation or property on the line for another? Well, to begin with he must have some faith that the person for whom he is willing to go good, will deliver on the promised act or promised restraint. To institute a system[14] of releasing a criminal where some responsible person in the community comes forward, at least in respect to the first offence, would, it seems to me, be of much benefit — not, just to the criminal at that moment, but for enumerable other people in their daily dealings with family, friends and associates. The business of gaining an ally before the need of one through a history of cooperation and fair dealing should be capital that a person might spend in a court of law. A person is to understand by his experiences that a criminal act hurtful to others will result in equal or comparable punishment to him. However, repeated past acts of kindness and consideration to others will get him off when once he made a mistake.

Lord MacMillan, in his introduction to Professor Leon Radzinowicz' work, in quoting the Irish historian and philosopher, William Lecky (1838-1903), was to write, as follows:

> To distinguish between crime that springs from strongly marked criminal tendency and crime that is due to mere unfavourable circumstances or transient passion or weakness of will; to distinguish among genuine criminal tenancies between those which are still incipient and curable and those which have acquired the force of an inveterate disease, is the basis of all sound criminal reform. It cannot be carried out without much careful classification and many lines of separate treatment. The agencies for reclaiming and employing juvenile criminals; the separate treatment of intoxication [and drug addiction]; the broad distinction drawn between a first offender and an habitual criminal; the prison regulations that check the contagion of vice, have all had a good effect in reducing the amount of crime. Most of these things cost much, but they produce a speedy and ample return. Money is seldom better or more economically spent than in diminishing the sum of human crime and raising the standard of human character.

The agencies to which Harold MacMillan referred in 1948 have diversified and multiplied and so has the cost. I am not so sure that any of it however has produced "a speedy and ample return." Fifty years have now passed and many of my fellow citizens are ready to express the sentiment that the sentencing of the convicted criminal has grown more and more ineffective, sentimental and meaningless. If the system we desire is one which converts the convicted criminal to a respectable law abiding citizen, and which — when such a conversion is not possible (this being, I suspect, the situation for the vast majority of cases) — is to deter the criminal from committing further crime, then we do not presently have the desired system in place. What we have, it seems, has failed in both departments, but most certainly has wholly failed to make crime difficult and unattractive.

———————————

"On Democracy."

Democracy is a tender topic for a writer: like motherhood and apple pie it is not to be criticized. One will risk being roundly condemned if he or she points out the serious bottleneck that is presented when a community attempts, through the democratic process, to set plans for positive social action. A man is not permitted to hesitate about its merits without the suspicion of being a friend to tyranny, a foe to mankind?[1]

The notions of government and of democracy are independent notions and do not, from what I can see of the case, depend on one another. What is likely required for the masses of people, as we see in "modern" world societies, is an established system of government. Where there is a need for an established system of government, it will likely naturally come about, doing so, whether or not it has the consent of the people, real or imagined. Putting aside for the moment the arguments of Hobbes and Locke, I believe, on the basis of plain historical fact, that governments come about naturally and maintain themselves naturally without the general will of the people. Indeed, I believe, with many others I suspect, that our long established democratic governments in the world (the United States and Canada being among them) did not come about by the general will of the people, at all; nor is it necessary that it should be maintained by the will of the people.[2] One should not conclude, therefore, that democracy is necessary for good government. It may not be. What is necessary for optimum prosperity is a state of acquiescence, which, as it happens, is the hallmark of western democracies. It may be, that the only thing needed is but the trappings of democracy.

An individual or group of individuals may take and maintain power by the use of coercive force. From the study of history we can see that this is the usual way by which power is gained, and maintained. However, it has long been understood that people might come together and explicitly agree to put someone in power. The best of the thinkers saw a process — call it democracy — by which groups might bloodlessly choose a leader. That each of the governed should have a say, or at least an opportunity to have a say, is a high flying ideal. But any system by which the peace is kept is an admirable system and democracy, such as it has evolved, has proven, in many cases, to be just such a system.

A precise definition of democracy might be had by consulting the *OED*. Democracy is government by the people; a form of government in which the sovereign power resides in the people as a whole, and is exercised either directly by them (as in the small republics of antiquity) or by officers elected by them. In modern use it vaguely denotes a social state in which all have equal rights, without hereditary or arbitrary differences of rank or privilege.

Walter Bagehot gave it a more uncelestial definition: "Each man is to have one twelve-millionth share in electing a Parliament; the rich and the wise are not to have, by explicit law, more votes than the poor and stupid; nor are any latent contrivances to give them an influence equivalent to more votes."

In considering the word, "democracy," what I first draw to your attention is the suffix, "-ocracy." This suffix expresses the operative meaning of the larger word, "democracy"; it is the indicator of the dominant, superior, or aspiring class who would rule; it is derived from the Greek word *kratos*, meaning strength or power. Any word might be added to this suffix, which will then indicate the type of rule, such as: plutocracy (rule by the wealthy), ochlocracy (mob-rule), angelocracy (government by angels), etc. Democracy is the rule by, or the dominion of, the people; it comes from the Greek word, *demos*. It is often referred to as popular government. Democracy, historically speaking, is to be compared with monarchy, rule of one; or with aristocracy, rule of the "best-born," or rule of the nobles.

Whatever its origins (and we will consider its origins) democracy has come to mean a principle or system to which most all political parties of the western world would subscribe, no matter their political beliefs. It is politics. It goes beyond the periodic act of voting. It is characterized by participation in government, where members of the community can involve themselves in governmental decisions, usually by allowing them to take part in anything at all which amounts to a public demonstration of popular opinion.

Grecian Democracy:

The first democracy, of which we have record, is that which was practiced in ancient Athens. In his capacity as a history writer, Aristotle, in his work, *The Athenian Constitution* (350 BC), wrote that the Athenians practiced democracy only to the extent of putting and keeping in power members of a very exclusive group, a group which formed but a minority in the universal group we stylize as society. The Athenian constitution was oligarchical, in every respect. The poorer classes were the serfs of the rich. They cultivated the lands of the rich and paid rent. The whole country was in the hands of nine magistrates, called *archons*, who were elected according to qualifications of birth and wealth. These ruling magistrates held their positions for life, except for that latter period when they served for a term of ten years. In time, this Greek notion of democracy was set aside in favor of the draw.

> ... the method of election in the choice of *archons* is replaced by lot; some way must be found to keep the rich from buying, or the knaves from smiling, their way into office. To render the selection less than wholly accidental, all those upon whom the lot falls are subjected, before taking up their duties, to a rigorous *dokimasia*, or character examination, conducted by the Council or the courts. The candidate must show Athenian parentage on both sides, freedom from physical defect and scandal, the pious honoring of his ancestors, the performance of his military assignments, and the full payment of his taxes; his whole life is on this occasion exposed to challenge by any citizen, and the prospect of such a scrutiny presumably frightens the most worthless from the sortition. If he passes this test the archon swears an oath that he will properly perform the obligations of his office, and will dedicate to the gods a golden statue of life-size if he should accept presents or bribes.

Durant in *Our Oriental Heritage* continued to write that the head man, the *archon basileus*, must "nine times yearly ... obtain a vote of confidence from the Assembly" and any citizen may bring him to task for an inappropriate act of his. "At the end of his term all his official acts, accounts, and documents" are reviewed by a special board, *logistai*, which is responsible to the Council. "Severe penalties, even death, may avenge serious misconduct."

Grecian democracy, however, such as it was, was soon covered over with the murk of the middle ages. Democracy's re-flowering in the world, in respect to the rights of the people, first appeared in England with the

Glorious Revolution of 1688. A study of an era known as *The Enlightenment*, is the study of the beginnings of modern democracy.[3]

The Enlightenment:

Out of the Dark Ages, in gradual awaking stirs, came the Age of Reason. The Enlightenment was fully established and growing vigorously by the 18th century. As the shackles of oppression, so firmly clamped on during the middle ages, became loose, men sought to apply reason to religion, politics, morality, and social life. With the coming of The Enlightenment men began to express their minds; no longer were men cowed by the great mystery of the universe and their minds, through ignorance, ruled by fears. The Enlightenment was a time when human beings pulled themselves out of the medieval pits of mysticism. It was a spontaneous and defused movement which fed on itself and led to the great scientific discoveries from which we all benefit today. Beliefs in natural law and universal order sprung up, which not only promoted scientific findings and advancements of a material nature, but which also drove the great political thinkers of the time, such as: Francis Bacon (1561-1626), Bernard Mandeville (1670-1733), Charles Louis de Secondat Montesquieu (1689-1755), Voltaire (1694-1766), Jean Jacques Rousseau (1712-88), David Hume (1711-76) and, of course the brightest political light of all, John Locke (1632-1704).

Representative Government:

In England, Edward the First, in 1295, with a view to dealing with his impecuniosity, issued a writ to the sheriff of Northhampton. The people, of all things, were refusing to pay taxes and they were becoming belligerent. Edward was getting advise to the effect that it might be better to sit down with the people, or rather their representatives, than to let loose the royal troops. Letting the troops loose would be an act which would destroy the country's riches, a share of which the king wanted for himself. Thus, we would have seen the royal messenger riding out from the king's castle to deliver this royal writ to the sheriff of Northhampton. This royal writ of Edward's had the Latin words, *elegi facis*, meaning that the persons who were to sit on the people's Council (the beginnings of parliament) were to be elected headmen such as the burgesses and knights, and they were to have "full and sufficient power for themselves and the communities" which they represent; they were to come to Council — ready, to conduct and to conclude the important business of the land.

Now, one of the most fundamental questions of politics — whether of 1295, or of modern day — is this: Should the representative, sent to the legislature — assuming, in the first place, that he or she has canvassed the subject to be voted upon and all the far flung consequences of it — vote the way the majority of his constituents would have him vote, or should he vote on the basis of what he thinks is right, no matter that it may run against the majority of what his constituents would like. Edmund Burke, a most brilliant political thinker, thought that the representative should vote his conscience.[4]

Parliament is not a congress of ambassadors from different and hostile interests; which interests each must maintain, as an agent and advocate, against other agents and advocates; but parliament is a deliberative assembly of one nation, with one interest, that of the whole; where, not local purposes, not local prejudices ought to guide, but the general good, resulting from the general reason of the whole. You choose a member indeed; but when you have chosen him, he is not a member of Bristol, but he is a member of parliament. ...

Your representative owes you, not his industry only, but his judgment; and he betrays instead of serving you if he sacrifices it to your opinion. ...

The state includes the dead, the living, and the coming generations.

The Dilemma of Representative Government:

Given human nature and the political process, full democracy, beyond the smallest group size, may simply not be workable, at all. Each of us has a right to cast a vote for an individual to represent us in the legislative assembly. The elected person then goes off to represent all of his constituents, whether they voted for him or not, indeed, whether they have even voted. How is he to look at issues and how is he to vote (assuming, for the moment, that he has a free vote in parliament). Should he vote on the basis of what he perceives the majority of his constituents want, right or wrong; or, as Burke suggests, does he vote his own conscience, vote as a "better and more informed person" than his average constituent; or does he, as it seems our system obliges, just vote the party line.

Representative institutions are of little value, and may be a mere instrument of tyranny or intrigue, when the generality of electors are not sufficiently interested in their own government to give their vote, or, if they vote at all, do not bestow their suffrages on public grounds, but sell them for money, or vote at the beck of someone who has control over them or whom for private reasons they desire to propitiate. Popular election, as thus practised, instead of a security against misgovernment, is but an additional wheel in its machinery.
— Mill.

The problem, as is so clearly set forth by Mill, is quite aside from the further and separate problem "that issues at stake in political life are too many and too complicated and that very many of them [issues] are actually unknown both to the representatives and to the people represented." (Leoni.)

It should be remembered, too, that any decision made and action taken in an assembly of "our" representatives can be done on the barest majority of a group; which might have been elected on the barest majority of a popular vote; which majority of a popular vote, might well, and usually does, represent a minority of the population. How can it ever be stated that any particular government measure will accord with the wishes of the majority?[5]

Democracy In Action:

In a monarchy, or, for that matter, any state where rule is carried out by a privileged class without consulting with the masses in any direct way, it was recognized, at least in the 18th and 19th centuries, that what was needed was a submissive, a confident and a stupid people. Such people in these earlier centuries existed in predominate numbers. Sadly, yet today, in the 21st century, it is rare, even in the western democracies, to find many people who are independently working through for themselves and taking fixed positions on important political concepts such as democracy, freedom and government. For democracy to work there must, as a prerequisite, be a people educated and be a people ready to inform themselves of the great issues which face them. Unfortunately, a politically educated public, this important ingredient to the proper working of democracy, is missing.

First off, it must be recognized, that the country is not run, at least not in between elections, with the executive checking with the people by way of referenda (as the Swiss do). However, the people who possess government power and who would like to keep it, are bound to proceed on the basis of popular opinion; the difficulty is that public opinion arises as a result of an agenda which is set by minority groups to which vote chasing politicians cow, a process which is generally aided and abetted by an ignorant press.

[Proper political conclusions] cannot be had by glancing at newspapers, listening to snatches of radio comment, watching politicians perform on television, hearing occasional lectures, and reading a few books. It would not be enough to make a man competent to decide whether to amputate a leg, and it is not enough to qualify him to choose war or peace, to arm or not to arm, to intervene or to withdraw, to fight on or to negotiate. ...

When distant and unfamiliar and complex things are communicated to great masses of people, the truth suffers a considerable and often a radical distortion. The complex is made over into the simple, the hypothetical into the dogmatic, and the relative into an absolute. ... the public opinion of masses cannot be counted upon to apprehend regularly and promptly the reality of things. There is an inherent tendency in opinion to feed upon rumors excited by our own wishes and fears. — Lippmann.

We should never hope or aim to choose a bully, but the elective process will give no guarantee that the people will not end up with one. Democracy, no matter its imperfections, is a way by which the people can bloodlessly turn out leaders; but the democratic process will only work with the consent of the leaders. The best that can be expected of a constitutional democracy, the best that can be expected by any political system, is a process by which the people turn up a leader or leaders which are prepared to deal with both the bullies amongst us and those at our borders. Hopefully, the leader or leaders, so turned up by the "democratic process," do not turn out to be a worst set of bullies than that which might exist in an ungoverned state. If, in the "democratic process," an elected leader turns into a bully, well then, though it may be an effective rallying cry, one should not rely on democracy to turn the bully out. To turn out a powerful bully, great quantities of spilt blood are needed.

Democracy, Government, and Freedom:

Democracy, in my view, is only compatible with a free economy; it can only exist, in substance, in an economy of ideas. Like a fish to water, democracy can only exist in a total atmosphere of freedom of action; it is completely incompatible with a system that provides for a governing authority with coercive power. If one accepts (anarchists, for example, do not) that a government, to some extent or other is necessary for a civilized society, then it is to be recognized that the business of governing (as apart from the business of electing representatives) cannot be conducted in a democratic manner. Lippmann deals with this problem:

> ... there has developed in this century a functional derangement of the relationship between the mass of the people and the government. The people have acquired power which they are incapable of exercising, and the governments they elect have lost powers which they must recover if they are to govern. What then are the true boundaries of the people's power?... They can elect the government. They can remove it. They can approve or disapprove its performance. But they cannot administer the government. They cannot themselves perform. They cannot normally initiate and propose the necessary legislation. A mass cannot govern.

Where mass opinion dominates the government, there is a morbid derangement of the true functions of power. The derangement brings about the enfeeblement, verging on paralysis, of the capacity to govern. This breakdown in the constitutional order is the cause of the precipitate and catastrophic decline of Western society. It may, if it cannot be arrested and reversed, bring about the fall of the West.

The notions of freedom and of democracy, we might reasonably conclude, rest on the same foundations. This is not the case for the concepts of government and freedom; they will have nothing to do with one another; they work against one another. The principal business of government is the taking of freedom away from people; it is how government achieves its ends.

The Press and Democracy:

To begin with, those charged with informing the public, such as our journalists, should very carefully examine the "expert evidence" that is thrown their way. Our government experts must be cross-examined and asked if they have any interest in the outcome? The answer is that most of them do — if, for no other reason, than they are in the pay of the government, as either bureaucrats lodged in the upper end of the government echelon, or those resting in publicly funded universities, or those who are in the social welfare business.

The result of the syndrome is predictable, for, as the public conflict grows, people come to doubt expert pronouncements. Normally people primarily judge the propositions before them in a most obvious way, by their source. For example, "Of course she claims oil spills are harmless — she works for Exxon." "Of course he says Exxon lies — he works for Nader." When established experts lose credibility, the demagogues take over and we are left in our mass democracy with groups trying to out-shout one another.

When their views have corporate appeal, they take them to the public through advertising campaigns. When their views have pork-barrel appeal, they take them to legislatures through lobbying. When their views have dramatic appeal, they take them to the public through media campaigns. Groups promote their pet experts, the battle goes public, and quiet scientists and engineers are drowned in the clamor.

Do the important issues get debated in the mass media? Some things seem to work well enough without any notice being taken by the public, often these are the most simple and important workings of society such as family cooperation. In the media, as in human consciousness, one concern tends to drive out another. This is what makes conscious attention so scarce and precious. Our society needs to identify the facts of its situation more swiftly and reliably, with fewer distracting feuds in the media. This will free public debate for its proper task — judging procedures for finding facts, deciding what we want, and helping us choose a path toward a world worth living in.

The People:

I now deal with the concept, "the people": and, in particular Burke's notion that it consists of not just the aggregate of living persons, but "those that are dead and those who are to be born."

That is why young men die in battle for their country's sake and why old men plant trees they will never sit under. ...

This invisible, inaudible, and so largely nonexistent community gives rational meaning to the necessary objectives of government.

If we deny it, identifying the people with the prevailing pluralities who vote in order to serve, as Bentham has it, "their pleasures and their security," where and what is the nation, and whose duty and business is it to defend the public interest? Bentham leaves us with the state as an arena in which factions contend for their immediate advantage in the struggle for survival and domination. Without the invisible and transcendent community to bind them, why should they care for posterity? And why should posterity care about them, and about their treaties and their contracts, their commitments and their promises. Yet without these engagements to the future, they could not live and work; without these engagements the fabric of society is unraveled and shredded.   — Lippmann.

Virtual Representation:

Edmund Burke was an exponent of "virtual representation." The idea is, that those who do not have the franchise or those who cannot have it by custom or law (i.e., for reasons such as they are infants, or indeed, are unborn), are, nonetheless, represented by those exercising government power. When one thinks it through, one is bound to come to the conclusion that it is pretty presumptuous to strike on a legislative course not knowing the degree or type of impact which such a course will have on those generations which stretch out (we hope) much beyond that time which will mark the current generation's departure from this life.

In the days prior to 1832, great large populated areas, for example, Manchester in England, were not represented by a seat in parliament while little villages, particularly in the south of England, had a seat, sometimes more than one. While the larger county seats were somewhat democratic, the little southern village seats were totally in the pockets of the local lords. The Great *Reform Bill of* 1832 fundamentally redefined the electoral districts, thus the end came for the pocket boroughs.[6] Since 1832,

Britain (and, thus, in modern day Canada) there exists a permanent commission on electoral boundaries.

All that I can see of democracy's role is to put into place those people, who, in a very general way, represent the views of the majority, or rather the views of the party to whom they owe their advancement. This of course is a recipe for oppression of the minorities no matter from which strata of society they come, and no matter whether any particular individual from within society likes the party policies, or not.

> The most difficult of all political problems is to be solved — the people are to be at once thoroughly restrained and thoroughly pleased. The executive must be like a steel shirt of the Middle Ages — extremely hard and extremely flexible. It must give way to attractive novelties which do not hurt ...   — Bagehot.

Is democracy workable? Can it work at all? For a free and democratic nation to work, a politician must, in the first place and right off the bat, in an honest fashion, convince the electorate that democracy is what they need, if they are to get what they want — optimal human conditions for the medium term. The reality of things, with no exceptions that I can think of, is that what people desire is the soft and the easy; what is needed is the hard and the difficult (if only to achieve the soft and the easy).

> Faced with these choices between the hard and the soft, the normal propensity of democratic governments is to please the largest number of voters. The pressure of the electorate is normally for the soft side of the equations. That is why governments are unable to cope with reality when elected assemblies and mass opinions become decisive in the state, when there are no statesmen to resist the inclination of the voters and there are only politicians to excite and exploit them.

> There is then a general tendency to be drawn downward, as by the force of gravity, towards insolvency, towards the insecurity of factionalism, towards the erosion of liberty, and towards hyperbolic wars. — Lippmann.

Much is asked of democracy: for while by definition no one within a democracy is to have special privileges; it, as a system, is to accommodate all groups of people, no matter how unalike they may be, one to the other. It may be that democracy can only work where the great mass of people are alike, or at least striving to be alike. This may be the reason why, through the years, democracy has worked so well in countries such as Canada and the United States. Historically, the United States (and Canada as well) was the great melting pot where newcomers came — their wish was to be American and to raise their children as Americans. However, there are now signs that democracy in our countries, as a system, is breaking down. More and more, it seems, there are groups, particularly in Canada, which arise and are no longer content to strive to stay in the common middle and share common ideals, but rather they diverge. This divergence, unfortunately, has been supported by government action in a combined effort to hold and promote distinctiveness of these existing and emerging groups.

Thus, democracy, as past experience will demonstrate, works only where the population shares, fundamentally, the same goals and aspirations. Historically, God and country have been the two banners under which the great masses could proudly stand, but in a modern society, God and country mean less and less, while at the same time the goals and aspirations of various groups increase and diverge. It maybe that democracy is, and indeed has always been unworkable, but we must continue to hold the ideal high and see to it that its trappings are securely fixed in place as a bulwark, such as it is, against tyrannical rule.[7]

The reality is that we are forever fixed with an oligarchy (government of the few) masquerading as a democracy. The purpose of the ruling few is to execute its constitutional functions, which, because of the difficulties with democracy, should be tightly circumscribed. The ideal of democracy is to be promoted to the rulers and the ruled as a sacred icon. Never mind that it cannot be used to put a society into action, to pass laws; never mind that it will rarely cast up honest and wise leaders. It is, in the final analysis, a system that will routinely and inexpensively rotate those in charge; a manner of bloodlessly changing the guard.

"The Theory of Government."

Herein I shall deal with questions about people and how they organize themselves under leadership, under rules for conduct, under government. The central questions asked by this paper are: What is government? And, What is a government's purpose, its powers, and its perils. Through the writings of the classic political thinkers, these and other questions of a collateral nature are examined. Collateral questions such as: How does government come about? Is it an automatic process, or an invention of man? What power does government have over a person? And who is it that sanctions this power? And for what purpose? Are there limits in the exercise of government power? And if there are limits, what, for the individual, are the practical problems and remedies when these limits are exceeded?

As David Hume expressed it, "one poison may be an antidote to another."[1] A touch of one, even with its sickly effect, may save the fatal consequence of another. Freedom is essential to the life of an individual. Without it the individual will wither; and withered parts are useless, indeed, a burden on the whole. A person, however, cannot have a licence to do anything he or she likes. Rules for behavior must be made and enforced, but not so much as to fatally poison freedom; but only a touch to preserve it. Thus, government is like a purifying poison, a stabilizer; needed, not for itself, but so to permit the highest level of individual freedom without anarchy.

To go into the Hobbesian and Lockeian theories about Pre-Social Man is more than I intend to do at this place. Suffice it to say that Thomas Hobbes (1588-1679) thought, in uncivilized times, in times before government, there existed continual war with "every man, against every man." This Hobbsian view is to be contrasted with that of John Locke (1632-1704). Locke thought that the original state of man was happy and was characterized by reason and tolerance. He thought that all human beings, in their natural state, were equal and free to pursue matters, considered as inalienable rights — life, health, liberty, and possessions. One will have to make up their own mind as to whether man has a natural morality, or not. However, I am bound to point out that Locke's theories on the nature of man have held sway for three hundred years. It was to be the middle of the 19th century before the theories of evolution (theories supported by hard facts) were to be discussed and accepted; Locke's views are consistent with evolutionary theory. That which distinguishes man from the animals, is man's capacity to communicate and cooperate with one another, a capacity which evolved slowly over millions of years and which could not possibly evolve in the "solitary and brutish" world which Hobbes thought existed.

To the individual, other than to himself, justice counts for nothing: what drives man, primitive or otherwise, is self-love. Man by his nature is driven to seek "power, ambition, lucre, lust"; and will take from others to achieve his goals, unless restrained. The principal constraint for any one individual is this: he does not want to lose what he has in the attempt in getting more; and, above all, he does not want, himself or his family, to get hurt — worse, yet, to lose his liberty, or his life. Primitive man had to spend, at least, as much of his wealth and his time defending himself as he would in taking away the wealth of others. He would be ahead, if only he could trade one off against the other. But how to do that? One way, it seems the only way, is to have every one, within striking distance, submit to a common power, such as a great king, one to be supported, to be made and to be kept powerful, so to fight off enemies from abroad.

"All join to guard what each desires to gain." Thus, it is this very same "self-love" that drives man to collect together under "government and laws."

Anarchy:

Most of us shudder to hear the word — anarchy.[2] It is as if one might be immediately picked up by the police by even thinking of it. It is, however, but a word, one which "describes a state where there is an absence of government. A theoretical social state in which there is no governing person or body of persons, but each individual has absolute liberty (without implication of disorder)." From the definition, as found in the *OED*, there is no "implication of disorder"; no matter, the writers through the ages have treated anarchy as if it invariably leads to disorder. An absence of government, it seems to have been concluded (generally on no evidence at all), would bring on a state of lawlessness. Thomas Carlyle thought anarchy to be "the hatefullest of things," and one of the most admirable thinkers of all time, Francis Bacon, associated "absolute anarchy" to that of "confusion."

The question of what it would be like to live in a state of anarchy, is one of the great philosophic questions of all times. On one side of this question, for example, was the French socialist, Pierre Joseph Proudhon who declared "that as man becomes morally mature the artificial restrictions of law and government can be dispensed with." (*Chambers*.) Proudhon dreamed of a state of nature where all property (to Proudhon "property was theft") belonged to the whole and that "perfect man" would take from the store of property only that which was needed, that all men "by nature and destination" are to be in a society where all would be equal and free, and have no need for a government as every one went about in a loving and sharing way. The critics answered that for such a state, as was visualized by Proudhon, a new race of mankind would first have to be regenerated. Until then, a state of anarchy was but a "delightful dream." This whole notion of the history of men moving towards a perfect state, under-pinned the philosophy of Marx and the Russian revolution of the early 20th century.[3] Collectivists or socialists do not normally ascribe to the notion that history lives and is inextricably moving, as if animate — to some glorious end state; indeed a person's disbelief in this is what distinguishes him from a communist. Both communists and socialists, however, believe, contra to the hard evidence of history, in the perfectibility of man.

One need not resort to choosing between Hobbes and Locke, or, indeed come to any hard conclusions as to the nature of man at all, in order to conclude first off, that anarchy would not work and that some level of government is needed for the better working of society. For man, as is crystal clear, is not perfect. If he be headed anywhere in particular, including to that of an angelic state, his estimated time of arrival be, at least, a millennium away. The fact is, however, that too much government, as an antidote to anarchy, will leave society as the patient, worse off.

Slavery results from laws, laws are made by governments, and, therefore people can only be freed from slavery by the abolition of governments. ... And it is time for people to understand that governments not only are not necessary, but are harmful and most highly immoral institutions, in which a self-respecting, honest man cannot and must not take part. ... And as soon as people clearly understand this, they will ... cease to give the governments soldiers and money. And as soon as a majority of people cease to do this, the fraud which enslaves people will be abolished. Only in this way can people be freed from slavery.   — Tolstoy.

Anarchy comes from the Greek; it means no law or supreme power. Anarchism exists where people, individually or by voluntary groups, are left to totally sort out their own affairs. Should this work? The answer might come when one studies the nature of man. At his center, at his heart, every man is an anarchist. He only wishes that his neigbour be governed. As for himself, he wishes but to be left alone.

Anarchism is a theory of the absolute and complete liberty of the individual. The wish, one that man has carried in his heart through the ages is that he should have no master but one that suits his own mood. It is the extreme of liberty; at the other end of the pole is totalitarianism, absolute control possessed by government, or, almost by definition, in one person (one can think of Bismarck, Hitler and Stalin, and the many others who, throughout the world, emulate them to this day).

Personally, I do not believe anarchism would likely work, though — while probably not the best way for society to conduct itself — anarchy is bound to be vastly superior to totalitarianism. In its scheme anarchism has one primary rule, and it is, "mind your own business." And under anarchism the primary crime is when one interferes with another's business.

It was Thomas Paine (1737-1809) who said, "The instant formal government is abolished, society begins to act. A general association takes place, and common interest produces common security." Thus, one might say that anarchism is a state of affairs that does not last, directly a government is done away with, it is almost immediately reformed, usually in its simplest cast.

For most of us, we need some order in our lives much before we can get on with leading it. We are not so much concerned with our own personal disorders, for presumably we have some control over ourselves, but primarily, we would like to bring the disorderly conduct of others under control. We have to know what to expect of them if we are to make our own plans. It is the activities of other persons with which we are concerned, activities which have potential to impact on us, for good or for bad.

Polity:

There is a word for order in a community of individuals, it is polity. Polity is the understanding of each, within the group, as to who is to do what. Polity is required in all groups, whether it is two friends out for a sail across the water, or a larger group such as a bunch of boy scouts out for a hike, or a very much larger group such as the millions which make up a nation. One should not conclude that a set of rules must be intentionally set down for polity to exist,[4] indeed, there is no need to think that government, as we know it, for the polity of a country (civil organization, or civil order) need exist at all. Anarchists think not, as we have seen. They believe that civil order might well be a spontaneous and natural event, just like the polity of bees. The prevailing opinion, however, is that government, at least to some degree, is needed to bring civil polity about.

Government is the continuous exercise of the power to control all the individuals that go to make up a community. Usually we think of this community as the whole of all those who live in some sort geographical area, the larger political units being sovereign countries. This government power is exercised by a body of persons who have become charged with the authority of governing. They may take charge by some voluntary arrangement, real or imagined, by all those within the community, or the governing group may well have seized government power by force. In many of the "primitive" governments, and I dare say in many of the smaller human groups found in society, a person will simply arise and be accepted as a leader because of his or her superior leadership abilities.

The commonwealth seems to me to be a society of men constituted only for the procuring, preserving, and advancing their own civil interests. Civil interests I call life, liberty, health, and indolency of body; and the possession of outward things, such as money, lands, houses, furniture, and the like. It is the duty of the civil magistrate, by the impartial execution of equal laws, to secure unto all the people in general and to every one of his subjects in particular the just possession of these things belonging to this life. If anyone presume to violate the laws of public justice and equity, established for the preservation of those things, his presumption is to be checked by the fear of punishment, consisting of the deprivation or diminution of those civil interests, or goods, which otherwise he might and ought to enjoy. But seeing no man does willingly suffer himself to be punished by the deprivation of any part of his goods, and much less of his liberty or life, therefore, is the magistrate armed with the force and strength of all his subjects, in order to the punishment of those that violate any other man's rights.

— John Locke.

Because of pure fear (it is an unproductive and an unhealthy state) people have, since the earliest times, preferred to band themselves together in a group under a strong leader. The principal fear from which people seek relief, is the fear of other people; either from within or from without the group.[5] The simple fact is that there exists other people, who might injure the group, or take their property, or — often in the same aggressive act — do both. In putting themselves under a leader strong enough to frighten off, or to deal with the victimizers of the world, the members within the group still continue to run a risk, the risk of being a victim to the leader, himself, but since the leader would like to stay in power, it is usually a lesser risk. At any rate, if the members are molested by the leader, they can expect that the molestations will come from only one source; and the abuse, harm, injury and plunder, in total, they hope, will be less than what the people would otherwise experience if they were not within the group under a strong leader.

(For thousands, and thousands of years it never struck the members of groups, nor hardly the leaders, that the members should have much say in the choice of the leader, or have a say in his continuing support. That the leader should be strong and not molest the members too badly, was good enough. Except for the Greeks and the Romans the idea of democracy for most people was just that, an idea; for many people of the world it is still just an idea. Historically, workable democracies, in a representative form, have only recently appeared on the world stage. Best now that I tell you to keep the notion of "democracy" separate from that of "government." The ideal known as democracy, may, in reality, exist or not, no matter — in its name bloodless revolutions come about and new governments are had [forget whether it makes any difference, or not]. My point is this: no matter how a government comes into being — democracy, or not — a given group needs a strong leader, one who, while not being a bully himself, can deal with the bullies of the world.)

What is it that we as individuals expect of government? Not much, I would assert, beyond the regulatory apparatus necessary to carry on national defence, and of maintaining public order and personal safety. If you are of a socialist bent — one, who might trace his views back to Plato through Hegel and up to Marx — then a broad and a somewhat limitless role is cast for government. At least this much we can all agree upon: government's role is to include the function of defence, of police, and (to a limited extend) to public health and other services which do not lend themselves to voluntary effort.[6] It was Bentham's view that, to these fixed categories, governmental functions should be so limited.

> With the view of causing an increase to take place in the mass of national wealth, or with a view to increase the means either of subsistence or enjoyment, without some special reason, the general rule, is, that nothing ought to be done or attempted by government. The motto, or watchword of government on these occasions, ought to be — Be Quiet; ... [And that government be well advised to that request] Diogenes made to Alexander: 'Stand out of my sunshine.' We have no need of favour — we require only a secure and open path.   — Bentham.

Wealth:

Bentham used the expression, "national wealth," and, we might ask, What is it? Simply, to beg the question, it is the sum of all the individual wealth in the nation. Carlyle thought that power is wealth. But, power itself is not wealth but rather the route to it. Henry George[7] gave a practical definition to the concept: wealth, according to George, "is all material things produced by human labor, having exchange value." A more ethereal meaning to wealth was given by the American writer, John Ruskin (1819-1900), when he declared what to him was a great fact, to be clearly stated — "there is no wealth but life."[8] After a short consultation with the *OED*, I came to the view, from the standpoint of the individual experiencing it, that wealth is the condition of being happy and prosperous. Note, that in its primary meaning, it, wealth, is a human feeling, a feeling of well-being. In its secondary meaning it connotes things in which material riches consist, goods and/or possessions. While it is by no means beyond controversy, it is in this last sense, the same sense taken by Henry George, that the "science" of economics takes its meaning of the word, wealth. Most economists use the word as a collective term for those things, the abundant possession of which, by individuals, constitute the riches and/or prosperity of a community.

But the most fruitful examination of the idea of wealth comes about when one focuses on what John Stuart Mill had to say about the matter (it is always fruitful to look to the writings of John Stuart Mill). Mill defines wealth as all things which possess exchangeable value. The objects which represent wealth need not necessarily be things which in themselves be useful or agreeable to the possessor, as long as the possessor thinks his properties are tradeable for such things as those that will bring him direct pleasure, or use; then, for him, such "useless" possessions are wealth. As any study of the notion will show, certain things can only have wealth to its possessor, such as those things which are gratuitously afforded by nature.[9]

Wealth, then, may be defined, as all useful or agreeable things which possess exchangeable value; or in other words, all useful or agreeable things except those which can be obtained, in the quantity desired, without labour or sacrifice. ... To an individual, anything is wealth, which, though useless in itself, enables him to claim from others a part of their stock of things useful or pleasant.   — Mill.

"The purpose of government," as Thomas Jefferson said, "is to allow for the preservation of life and liberty, and the pursuit of happiness." (*The Federalists Papers.*) (Note the use of the words "allow" and "pursuit.") Government cannot give life, it cannot give liberty, and it cannot give happiness; it can only take such things away. Liberty, or freedom, is a topic which arises in any discussion concerning government. It arises, not because government can contribute to freedom, in any way, but rather because government invariably, due to its very nature, encroaches on freedom. Government is to be treated as a trained guard dog, to be led out into the crowd by its handlers under strict control and sharp command. Usually the mere presence of Government power is enough to remind people to leave the liberty of others alone so that each person, unfettered in any way except by proper law, through individual choice, might create wealth, and to use it or preserve it, as they should choose. Only the individual, each in his own way, can create wealth; and by individuals doing this does the wealth of the nation come about. Wealth thus comes about because people have the freedom to choose, in every instance, what they individually calculate is best for them; the trillions of individual decisions that freely occur every day in our economy is what keeps us all going. To maintain an environment in which exchanges between people, within the law, voluntarily occur: this

— if the goal is to increase the store of wealth in the country — is the sole function of government. It is there to punish the citizen who encroaches on the freedom of another, government's role is as a referee, it must stay clear of the play. It must leave the business of creating wealth to those who can do it, to those that can only do it, to those outside of government. Government cannot create wealth it can only destroy it.

I quote John Stuart Mill:

The object of this essay [*On Liberty*] is to assert one very simple principle, ... that the sole end for which mankind are warranted, individually or collectively, in interfering with the liberty of action of any of their number, is self-protection. That the only purpose for which power can be rightly exercised over any member of a civilized community, against his or her will, is to prevent harm to others.

Frédéric Bastiat:

If every person has the right to defend — even by force — his person, his liberty, and his property, then it follows that a group of men have the right to organize and support a common force to protect these rights constantly. This principle of collective right — its reason for existing, its lawfulness — is based on individual right. And the common force that protects this collective right cannot logically have any other purpose or any other mission than that for which it acts as a substitute. Thus, since an individual cannot lawfully use force against the person, liberty, or property of another individual, then the common force — for the same reason — cannot lawfully be used to destroy the person, liberty, or property of individuals or groups.

Some among us have the notion that government fulfills a need of human society for a "directive apparatus." We do not need government for this reason. Assuming puny men could figure out how to construct such an apparatus, the cost would be immense. And what for? The whole event happens automatically. Society is quite capable of running itself and as the beating of a heart, and just as essential, no thought need be given to the topic. Production and distribution of all valuable goods and services in society are ultimately brought on by and through the voluntary co-operation of most every one. We do it through the operation of contract, a most powerful legal concept. "Demand and supply, and the desire of each man to gain a living by supplying the needs of his fellows, spontaneously evolve that wonderful system whereby a great city has its food daily ... in multitudinous varieties ... while the quantities of the numerous commodities required daily in each locality are adjusted without any other agency than the pursuit of profit." (Herbert Spencer.)

In dealing with the question — What is the purpose of government? I am obliged to point out its loftiest duty: and that is to instill, primarily by example, the great personal virtues that need to be prevalent in the huge herd that is to be governed. Necessary not only so we can all get along better with one another, but, primarily — and here I refer directly to the Confucian notion of good government[10] — so as to make the governed follow its legitimate directives, willingly and without the expense and destruction of compulsive government force. The muck and mire in which an over-extended government invariably finds itself is hardly conducive to the exercise of this lofty duty of setting a good example. An over-extended government is invariably obliged to resort to the use of force.

Authority intoxicates,
And makes mere sots of magistrates;
The fumes of it invade the brain,
And make men giddy, proud, and vain ...:
By this the fool commands the wise,
The noble with the base complies,
The sot assumes the rule of wit,
And cowards make the brave submit.
— Butler.

... he who wields it [power] is often but the puppet of circumstances, like the fly on the wheel that said, "What a dust we raise!" It is easier to ruin a kingdom and aggrandize one's own pride and prejudices than to set up a greengrocer's stall. An idiot or a madman may do this at any time, whose word is law, and whose nod is fate. Nay, he whose look is obedience, and who understands the silent wishes of the great, nay easily trample on the necks and tread out the liberties of a mighty nation ...
— William Hazlitt, "On Great and Little Things."

Power:

Power is an odious thing, we generally can smell it a long way off; those who wield it are automatically disliked. Our personal level of contentment, and therefore, I imagine the general level of contentment in society, is directly proportionate to the number of those who exert power over us. For this reason alone there would be good reason to severely limit the power of government. But there are much better reasons — but I run ahead of myself.

What is power? In its simplest definition, power is the ability to act upon a person and make them do something. Power, as Locke explained, is twofold: it can either be active or be passive. It is active when one exercises power by the threat of using force, or of the actual use of force. However, one may get another to do something, not through force, but rather through argument, by reason and by example. One uses passive power to get another to do something because ultimately it is in the best interest of the doer, himself, to do or not to do something: this is passive power. One uses passive power to show another that to take or to refrain from a certain action will ultimately advance the welfare of the person to whom the explicit or implicit request is being made. An exercise of passive power comes about when the doer is convinced without the threat or the application of force. Passive power is continually exercised by all of us, every day. We, to one degree or another, continually exercise power over ourselves and over all of our acquaintances. Passive power is asserted and met without any interference in the liberty of anyone, otherwise it would not be passive power. Passive power is the peaceful manner in which humans have evolved and by which they continue to sustain their lives. However, active power is another matter. The fundamental law is that no one may use active power except only in the defense of his person, his family and his property. It is this power that we delegate to government, for its use, almost exclusively. Government is to use the threat of force or actual force, strictly, and only against those in the community who have chosen to break the law, criminal law, as carefully and as fully defined as is possible.

As a civilized society we are obliged to proceed on this basis: that which "cannot be compassed by reason, wisdom and discretion" is something that is outside the law.[11] Government has a right to use force against those who are outside the law. The only moral (and practical) object in the use of force, generally, is to use it as a defense against one who is using it offensively, or it is apprehended that they are immediately about to do so. It is an individual's right to meet force with force. Each one of us, according to the teachings of Locke has this right. This right is impliedly granted to government, however, it is a reversionary right. If government uses it in any other way but in a defensive way, then government, by Lockian theory, loses the right to use force; it loses its legitimate power.

In all of this we cannot lose sight of the purpose of government, a topic with which I have previously dealt. Let me, in my reminder, once again, resort to the "Philosopher of Freedom," John Locke. I quote from his Second Treatise:

The great and chief end, therefore, of men's uniting into commonwealths, and putting themselves under government, is the preservation of their property. ... Men when they enter into society give up ... liberty [of a kind] ... yet it being only with an intention in every one the better to preserve himself, his liberty and property, [the power thus conferred] can never be supposed to extend farther than the common good, but is obliged to secure every one's property... [This power] is limited to the public good of the society. It is a power that hath no other end but preservation, and therefore can never have a right to destroy, enslave, or designedly to impoverish the subjects... To this end it is that men give up all their natural power to the society they enter into, and the community put the legislative power into such hands as they think fit, with this trust, that they shall be governed by declared laws, or else their peace, quiet, and property will still be at the same uncertainty as it was in the state of Nature. ... It cannot be supposed that they should intend, had they a power so to do, to give any one or more an absolute arbitrary power over their persons and estates, and put a force into the magistrate's hand to execute his unlimited will arbitrarily upon them; this were to put themselves into a worse condition than the state of Nature, wherein they had a liberty to defend their right against the injuries of others, and were upon equal terms of force to maintain it, whether invaded by a single man or many in combination. Whereas by supposing they have given up themselves to the absolute arbitrary power and will of a legislator, they have disarmed themselves, and armed him to make a prey of them when he pleases. ... It is true governments cannot be supported without great charge, and it is fit every one who enjoys his share of the protection should pay out of his estate his proportion for the maintenance of it. But still it must be with his own consent — i.e., the consent of the majority, giving it either by themselves or their representatives chosen by them; for if any one shall claim a power to lay and levy taxes on the people by his own authority, and without such consent of the people, he thereby invades the fundamental law of property, and subverts the end of government. For what property have I in that which another may by right take when he pleases to himself?

The most serious problem with power, to which Lord Acton referred, and which is quite separate from the aggravation of dealing with besotted magistrates, is, that it corrupts.[12] Read history and one will see that it is the rare leader who did not become corrupted. Trust in God, or trust in professionalism; neither will help. Put the best possible person in charge and often what one will end up with is the worst possible problem. There is a Latin proverb which I ran across in one of my law books and which covers the situation: *Optima corrupta pessima* (The best things, corrupted, become the worst). Given the choice, then, the best thing, as Thomas Jefferson pointed out, is to "guard against corruption and tyranny ... before they shall have gotten hold of us. It is better to keep the wolf out of the fold than to trust to drawing his teeth and talons after he shall have entered." This, dear reader, is a separate and a distinct argument for keeping government down to the barest of minimums.

In any analysis of governmental power, the question soon comes to mind — How is it, that government can maintain its power? How is it, as David Hume observed, "the many are governed by the few?"

The slaves of custom and established mode,
With pack horse constancy, we keep the road
Crooked or straight, through quags or thorny dells,
True to the jingling of our leader's bells
— Cowper.

The power of the state comes out from the willingness of the people to obey — Why do they obey, and at what point will they not obey? It was Hume who expressed surprise of the easiness with which 'the many are governed by the few'; those who govern have the force of opinion on their side, forget whether the opinion is right or wrong.   — Edmund Burke.

Why people obey government, and often obey government to the point of ruin, is a puzzling question. It may be simply a mystery, which we will assign simply to the powerful workings of custom and the mesmerizing effect of the "jingling bells" of the demigods — Who knows? There is little evidence that the crowd, the mob, the great unwashed,[13] has any political sense of things. Legal scholars have this idea that people follow government because, to do so, is constitutionally correct — never mind that the mass of people have no conscience thought about the process, at all; government has authority because, as we have seen, the people voluntarily give (in a constructive sense) this limited authority to government. This authority is not permanently given, it is but lent, and the grant and its limits are to be found in the country's constitution, something each country has, whether it is written down somewhere or not.

So, it is the country's constitution from which the government takes its power. It uses its constitutional power to make laws and to enforce them. A government cannot ever exceed the authority granted to it by the constitution. A constitution by its very nature will limit the authority of government — at least to this extent: government in its law making function can make no law which has the effect of abrogating *Natural Law*; and government, at all times, must put itself under the *Rule of Law*.

Natural Law & The Rule of Law:

The subject of legal philosophy is a subject for old men at law schools, and, if you have come this far with me, I do not want to lose you now, but, for any thinking citizen, some basic concepts must be considered.

First off, let me quickly touch on the Rule of Law. The law, whatever that maybe, is there for all to obey, including those in government. The Rule of Law is a doctrine which is derived from theories of Natural Law (the next following subject). In English law, the Rule of Law is a concept which has been used as a mechanism to control government power; it is a tool used exclusively by the courts.

And now, more generally we ask, What is the law? It has been and continues to be a much studied subject, but a quick, short and authoritative definition is this: law is "a rule of conduct imposed by authority." Normally, we think of this authority to be a person or persons, but it need not be. There do exist laws of an unearthly authority; laws which one might attribute to God, or more simply to nature. These laws exist entirely independent of man. They were around before man came on the scene and will be around long after he takes his ignoble exit. "That part of God's Law which bindes alwayes, bound before it was written and that is the law of nature." (John Donne.) I write of scientific laws, such as those that were discovered by the likes of Copernicus, Galileo, etc.

From brilliant human minds, through the reasoning process, came descriptions of natural relationships, natural laws.[14] Scientists do not create a thing, they describe that which exists. So, a natural law is descriptive, and, I should not have to add, cannot be broken by man. The fact is that natural law, to the extent possible, must be brought into account for all calculations; one must proceed in harmony with it or suffer the consequences. Natural law has neither been brought into force by human beings, nor can it be enforced by them; it has automatically brought them to the state in which they exist. Now, while natural law is not something that anyone of us thinks about too much, we all pretty well live in accordance with it. One must eat to live. One must grow or hunt for food. As part of this process, one must plan ahead and one must work. "Self-preservation is the very first and fundamental law of nature." (George Berkeley, 1685-1753.)

On the other hand, a prescriptive law is a rule of conduct imposed by the authority of government, a rule which has been decided upon by a human being or human beings. It imposes a relationship that does not naturally exist (otherwise why bother). It is a law that comes purely out of the human imagination. It can never run contrary to a natural law (at least not for long), and by its nature, can be broken by man. (Examples of prescriptive laws would be those that require that one must stop at a red light, or one must pay taxes.) The outcome in any contest between natural law and prescriptive law is inevitable. The best that can be expected by those who support prescriptive law that runs contra to natural law, is that the inevitable outcome might be delayed, but only at a considerable cost, usually in human misery and blood.

Before proceeding, we are obliged, for analytical purposes, to break prescriptive law down into a third level consisting of two categories: restrictive law and positive law. A restrictive law is a law which directs a person or persons not to do something; and positive law is a law that obliges one or more to do something. "Do not litter," is a example of a restrictive law, it always has a negative; this, as opposed to, "Pick up your litter," which, of course, is a example of positive law.

(Canada, as is the case in most all of the countries in the world, has taken to passing prescriptive laws, most of it in the worst form, as positive laws. One would think that such a fundamental question as to the type of laws a country is empowered to pass would be covered by its constitution — and I would argue that there is little room in the British constitution for positive law [a constitution which, with its common law heritage has been adopted by Canada] — but, at any rate, our free spending politicians and the social engineers on the payroll have paid little heed to the Canadian constitution, whatever it may be. The fact of the matter is, that, whether in pursuit of constitutional goals, or not, there has been a pouring out from our law making assemblies of prescriptive law in great smothering quantities, particularly, in the last twenty-five years. Most all of this legislative law has been in the nature of positive law, made in pursuit of the great delusion that we can cure all the difficulties of mankind by legislation.[15] Not only have our "elected representatives," *qua* legislators, passed, [driven by pressures brought on by all sides] huge volumes of written law, but they have given off this power [as if they can?] to their "unelected" bureaucratic friends who have run with it in great style, loading up on all and sundry, further and much more extensive volumes of governmental regulations. Regulations made by bureaucrats under the authority of a particular act are, neither made openly like acts of the legislature, nor are they published and distributed in the same way. This domain of "government regulations" is a vast area of law, hidden and dangerous. More than enough of it is substantive law, that is law that effects the rights of citizens. Now, mind you, any citizen might, with enough money and perseverance, go up against government, test "a regulation" before a court of law, and, I believe, in the majority of instances, the judge would likely throw the offending regulation out the nearest court window; but the realization of what a judge would likely do with most of their regulations does not deter government bureaucrats from grinding out regulation after regulation, much of it substantive law, much of it harmful to our fundamental rights. As to what kind of laws legislators are allowed by our constitution to pass, is an area, I submit, which desperately needs constitutional protection. For, as we can see from the experience of the last twenty-five years, or so, our trusted leaders, the ones we elected, have exercised little control over themselves and have created a huge economic problem for the country which has caused much greater problems than any of the problems which the legislation was designed to cure.)

Separation of Powers:

How to control or check government power was a question which a Frenchman by the name of Montesquieu pondered back in 1748.[16] Montesquieu thought the best way to limit government power is to particularize the power into distinct parishes, and then, in turn, to assign these parishes of power to the appropriate departments of government. This control mechanism recommended by Montesquieu might be best illustrated by the kind of control mechanism that exist in the control of nuclear missiles. My understanding of it is that no one person can launch such a missile. There are, I believe, three responsible persons each equipped with a key, each duty bound to check the "codes" before personally inserting and turning the key. Montesquieu, and the political thinkers who followed him (noteworthy are the framers of the American constitution of 1787), were anxious to see the existence of a controlling apparatus, so that raw government power should not fall into the hands of a power hungry individual or group of power hungry individuals. Government was to be broken down into three functions: executive, legislative, and judicial. A member of the government in one of these functions has full power but only within his appointed function. One department (legislative) is to make the laws, another (executive) is to run the country under the laws and another (judicial) is to enforce the laws against all. It is a fine idea, and we can see the trappings of it in most governments that exist in the world today. What needs to be asked is whether it functions as it was imagined it might. This is a topic which I cannot examine here at this place, but there are a number of questions to ask, including what impact the party system has on the separation of powers?

Having determined that we need government, it follows, government must have the authority to make laws, and the power to enforce them. Being that "every law is an infraction of liberty," (Bentham) it follows that the mere existence of government is an infraction on the liberty of those to be governed. The degree of encroachment of our freedom (the right to choose) is proportionate to the degree of our suffering in life. The right to choose is a life sustaining right; curtail it and you curtail life. The greater number of laws and the bigger the government, is all the worse for us. It is of extreme importance that we check government and have in mind continually the fact that government takes its authority and power from the citizens, us. This authority and power is usually found to be granted in the constitution of the country. We should, by our constitution, give no more authority and power than what is absolutely necessary to suit *our* purposes; to achieve *our* goals.

As we have seen, in our analysis, the reason people band together under government is so that they will not be abused, harmed, injured and/or plundered of their goods by those people, marauders, either from within or without the country, who would run amok without the threat of government force to keep them in check. Government, according to John Locke, will lose its right to exercise its power, however, when government abuses its people worse than any imaginable group of marauders that might be operating in the absence of a government. (At least without government, a person might take steps to deal with marauders, steps a person might not take when of the mistaken view that their interests were being protected by government.) Further, in Lockian theory, if government abuses the exercise of the power given it by the people, why then, the people have a natural right to rebel, as did the people of New England in 1776. A legitimate government, for its continued existence must limit itself to those matters that are common to all the members within the community, and only those matters, for example, matters such as civil and national defence. I fear, that here in Canada, government, on a regular basis now, involves itself in matters that are not common to all the members, but rather to particular groups, officially pitting one against the other and justifying their acts of plunder in the name of "social justice," a most ambiguous and obscure expression.

Of course, there are those among us, unfamiliar as they are with history, who still hold leaden socialistic thoughts, who really do believe that the answer to the big government disease is to increase the dose of the big government cure. They have come out and have declared they stand full square for all that which is good and just. These idealists also declare, in the very same breath that realists can have no such notions. They have cast themselves in the role of the deliverer of succor to all those who suffer in mankind. Now, to remedy injustices is an admirable goal, one that any thinking person, I should think, would share — but assuming that we will know an injustice when we see one, by what method shall we go about curing it? Shall we commit an injustice with the view to curing an injustice? A person can scarcely be held to be credible when he expresses that he has the ability to see how much effect will follow so much cause when he or she declares that he or she has the ability of dealing with social complexities of an extremely involved kind. But our elected assemblies are full of such people who by their actions profess to have such abilities; or who, and this is likely more the case, are led around by people whom they believe have such astounding abilities. The plain fact is that legislation lets loose additional factors creating, more often than not, further problems, often more serious than the problems it was intended that the legislation should cure. There then follows a compounding effect as the legislators pass more laws with the view to getting at the "legislative mischief" which was set in motion with the earlier legislation. All of this legislation has attending costs, not the least of which is the enormous labor we expend annually on our law making and law enforcing machinery.[17] But as serious as this expense is to the economic health of our country, it is not as serious as the additional and axiomatic problem which comes about when there is too much legislation; it brings all law, to an increasing degree, into disrepute. When people have no respect for the law, it matters not how many policemen you have, civilized society breaks down; anarchy will follow.

Thus government puts us all at great peril.[18] Government can cause injustices; it can waste valuable resources; it can bring our necessary laws into disrepute; it can lose its authority and let the country fall into anarchy, with the result of much misery and loss of life. All of this cries out for constitutional limits on governmental power. For the protection of all its citizens, government by a country's constitution should be set up along very simple and limited lines, one that can be continuously monitored and automatically checked.

What is needed for a country, for its own protection and for its stable and efficient operation, most every one will agree, is a strong government; but one which is constitutionally restricted to its proper and very limited role (basically to respond to the criminals who operate both within and from without a country's borders). The passing of laws (legislation) having a provision for the use of government force, is also to be constitutionally circumscribed. It is to be abhorred, whenever an individual in society is forced to give in to the desires of those who have set themselves up as knowing, Platonically, what is best for every one else. The theory that the community is to permit government to use force with a view to uniting all its citizens and by so doing make them share together the benefits which each individually can confer on the community, for the benefit of the community — while attractive in its statement, is a false theory. It is demonstratively an unworkable theory, which throughout history has been tried in practice, time and time again, and the result is always the same. A totalitarian state emerges and causes immense misery to all within the state. When, in its legislation, in its use of force, government suppresses the welfare of the individual, when its efforts are aimed to foster the attitude that one should not proceed to please oneself, then government commits a fatal error in the achievement of its laudable object, the betterment of the whole. The essential problem in proceeding in this manner is that individuals cannot contribute to the whole, indeed will be a drain on the whole, unless they are allowed to be free and productive, that is to say allowed to suit themselves. Human beings are not robots. They did not come to possess the independent spirit, so characteristic of man, by serving others. A person is not a fixed entity; he came about through an evolutionary process. He is a superior being because of the exercise of free choice. And, free choice continues to be essential to the individual's life and the life of a civilized community.

———————————

"Politics & The Lie of Legitimacy."

Tell potentates, they live
Acting by others' action;
Not loved unless they give,
Not strong, but by a faction ...
— Sir Walter Raleigh.

There can be nothing more important, when handing over government power to them, than to have a system which will turn up honest and able persons. Democracy, or that which we claim is such, whatever claims might be made in support of it, is, as will be shortly illustrated, not a system which turns up honest and able persons. Democracy is the rule by or the dominion of the people over the people. As a practical matter the masses cannot be called together to set and enforce the rules. Direct democracy, while tried in certain small republics of antiquity, is not what any modern democratic state has in place (Switzerland, I think, is the country which comes the closest to the ideal). The people like shareholders in a company elect officers to do the job of governing. This is known as representative democracy, and it is the art of politics that advances persons into these representative positions.

In a democracy there exists a political market. Politicians chase votes and electors chase government largesse. It is a myth that politicians promote the general interest; they are primarily interested in gaining and holding political office; it is power they seek. It is the political market that drives politically interested people to create and accommodate a coalition of special interests rather than the general interest. A quote from Walter Lippmann will illustrate the point:

In government offices which are sensitive to the vehemence and passion of mass sentiment public men have no sure tenure. They are in effect perpetual office seekers, always on trial for their political lives, always required to court their restless constituents. They are deprived of their independence. Democratic politicians rarely feel they can afford the luxury of telling the whole truth to the people. And since not telling it, though prudent, is uncomfortable, they find it easier if they themselves do not have to hear too often too much of the sour truth. The men under them who report and collect the news come to realize in their turn that it is safer to be wrong before it has become fashionable to be right.

With exceptions so rare that they are regarded as miracles and freaks of nature, successful democratic politicians are insecure and intimidated men. They advance politically only as they placate, appease, bribe, seduce, bamboozle, or otherwise manage to manipulate the demanding and threatening elements in their constituencies. The decisive consideration is not whether the proposition is good but whether it is popular — not whether it will work well and prove itself but whether the active talking constituents like it immediately. Politicians rationalize this servitude by saying that in a democracy public men are the servants of the people.

This devitalization of the governing power is the malady of democratic states. As the malady grows the executives become highly susceptible to the encroachment and usurpation by elected assemblies; they are pressed and harassed by the higgling of parties, by the agents of organized interests, and by the spokesmen of sectarians and ideologues. The malady can be fatal. It can be deadly to the very survival of the state as a free society if, when the great and hard issues of war and peace, of security and solvency, of revolution and order are up for decision, the executive and judicial departments, with their civil servants and technicians, have lost their power to decide.[1]

The Vote:

The great challenge is to keep people out of government who have no business, being in it. Democracy, for all its vaunted virtues, has been a dismal failure in getting proper people, I mean those with an understanding of the science and art of it, at the head of government. One of the principal difficulties of democracy is that it offers up no mechanism by which the brightest and the best become our leaders.[2] (How to achieve this goal, in keeping with our notions of democracy, is a subject which I hardly have room to treat at this place. Though for starters, I'll say this much: doctors, lawyers and other professionals spend years before they become licensed to deal with the problems of a particular individual. Any fool with a glib tongue and the right connections might end up with the government levers in his hands and thereby effect the welfare of hundreds of thousands of people. Persons should not be allowed to stand for political offices [which offices for this purpose should be graded in some fashion] unless and until they are tested in such things, as for example, elementary principles of political philosophy and constitutional law.) As it is, our leaders in our western democracies if not the brightest and the best are, at least, or so it is thought, the choice of the people.[3] Assuming for the moment that they are freely chosen by the people (a very doubtful proposition), the reality is, that the successful politician who climbs to the pinnacles of power[4] does so not because of any refined understanding of the role of government. Rather, he has arrived at his postion on account of his ability to attract those in charge of the election apparatus. This and through the devious means which are thought to be necessary, so as to be presented as an attractive "choice" to a majority of the voters.[5]

There have only ever been but a few countries, in all of history, in all of the world, where arrangements were, or are made, for those who go to make up a country's population, to vote for those who are to represent them in the government of their country. Even England, that great bastion of democracy, as the 19th turned into the 20th century, allowed but a part of the population to vote (women and non-property owners, for example, had no vote). These days, at least in the "western democracies," we all have the vote.

One is precluded from arguing that this is not a good idea. Certainly, Bentham in his work, published in 1789, didn't think to question the proposition that only certain people should have the vote.

> Men who would not be thought fit to be electors, are those who cannot be presumed to possess political integrity, and a sufficient degree of knowledge. Now we cannot presume upon the political integrity of those whom want exposes to the temptation of selling themselves; nor of those who have no fixed abode; nor of those who have been found guilty in the courts of justice of certain offences forbidden by the law. We cannot presume a sufficient degree of knowledge in women, whom their domestic condition withdraws from the conduct of public affairs; in children and adults beneath a certain age; in those who are deprived by their poverty of the first elements of education, &c. &c.

The fact of the matter is that with "universal suffrage," all too often, what we end up doing is putting people in positions of power whose only talent is that which is required to get themselves elected.[6] The question is, Who is capable of casting an informed vote? It is thought that minors are not. And yet — it has been my experience — that a good number of minors are capable, and indeed, have analyzed policy questions to some considerable degree. Why shouldn't they have the vote. Why do some certifiably insane persons have the vote, or those who know nothing of governing and care less about the subject. It was Schiller who observed: "Sense has ever been centered in the few. ... Votes should be weighed, not counted. The state must sooner or later be wrecked where the majority rules and ignorance decides." Who should have the vote is perhaps a political question long since dead, but, if it is a dead question, then all the more reason to keep the sphere of government action within areas that are strictly circumscribed.

We may well question the ability of the typical voter,[7] if they do it at all, to cast a vote on one side of a studied issue. However, it is not just the voter that is typically ignorant, unfortunately, all too often, so is the politician who stands for election.[8] Quite a number of us well appreciate this. And so, at each election there is a concerted effort to turn out one set of politicians who have abundantly illustrated their ineptitude; only to be fixed, post election, with another set which soon demonstrate they are no better than the last set. (Great expense, I might add, is incurred, as each new set goes about undoing the work of the previous set, the term I have come to use is "democratic fibrillation.") What is necessary is for us to come to grips with the great mythology of our age. Professor Leoni:

> No solemn titles, no pompous ceremonies, no enthusiasm on the part of applauding masses can conceal the crude fact that both the legislators and the directors of a centralized economy are only particular individuals like you and me, ignorant of 99 percent of what is going on around them as far as the real transactions, agreements, attitudes, feelings, and convictions of people are concerned. ... The mythology of our age is not religious, but political, and its chief myths seem to be 'representation' of the people, on the one hand, and the charismatic pretension of political leaders to be in possession of the truth and to act accordingly ...

Never mind the typical "western democracy" is a system that is run by demagogues, it is simply not participatory, though some may think the opportunities exist. Nor can it be labeled as participatory when only a third of the voters bother to get out. The fact is that "the participation of individuals in the law-making process has ceased to be effective and has become more and more a sort of empty ceremony taking place periodically in the general election of a country." (Leoni.)

It is in the nature of government to have a few tell the rest what it is that should be done, or, to put it on a proper footing, what is not to be done. By the normal democratic process, where there is disagreement (just about every time) then a vote is called and those who win by a simple majority[9] overrule the rest. It is a myth that every citizen has an equal weight with every other. Assuming all citizens have a vote (children, for example, do not); and only half of them bother to vote; and the election is won by 51% — then, those who parade around after the election declaring themselves the winners, may, indeed, have the real support of but only 25% of the electorate (assuming that this 25% knew what it was they were voting for in the first place); though, they claim the power to bind 100% of the citizens over to their ideas (legislation).

Professor Leoni, in his brilliant work, *Freedom and the Law* illustrates the tyranny of majority rule:

> ... when we consider the analogy at closer quarters, we realize that in assuming that 51 voters out of 100 are "politically" equal to 100 voters, and that the remaining 49 (contrary) voters are "politically" equal to zero (which is exactly what happens when a group decision is made according to majority rule) we give much more 'weight' to each voter ranking on the side of the winning 51 than to each voter ranking on the side of the losing 49.

In any event, Truth Cannot be Put to a Vote: Truth does not care for majoritarianism or egalitarianism. One cannot claim to have arrived at a knowledgeable position because 51 percent of the public agrees with you. It was Bruno who observed: "It is proof of a base and low mind for one to wish to think with the masses or majority, merely because the majority is the majority. Truth does not change because it is, or is not, believed by a majority of the people." And, George Santayana: "Most men's conscience, habits, and opinions are borrowed from convention and gather continually comforting assurances from the same social consensus that originally suggested them."

The Party System:

Men thinking freely will, in particular instances, think differently. But still, as the greater Part of the measures which arise in the course of public business are related to, or dependent on, some great leading general principles in Government, a man must be peculiarly unfortunate in the choice of his political company if he does not agree with them at least nine times in ten. If he does not concur in these general principles upon which the party is founded, and which necessarily draw on a concurrence in their application, he ought from the beginning to have chosen some other, more conformable to his opinions. ... How men can proceed without any connection at all is to me utterly incomprehensible.

— Edmund Burke.

The two-party system, indeed the cabinet form of government, evolved in England during the reigns of the first two Georges (1714-60).[10] George the First was a German prince, who, through a political arrangement, so as to shut out the Stuarts in England, was invited to sit on the English throne. George Macaulay Trevelyan, professor of History at Cambridge:

The outstanding fact in political history under the first two Georges is the obeyance of the Tory party as an effective force in Parliament. The two-party system did not die but it slept. There were always avowed Tories in Parliament, but they were not numerous enough either to take over the government when a change was needed, or to act alone as an Opposition. They usually worked with the section of the Whigs who happened to be opposed in the Whig Government of the day. Since there was no rival party which the Whig aristocracy as a whole had cause to fear, it grew negligent of public opinion, and relied more and more on perfecting the corrupt machinery of elections, instead of appealing on points of principle to the electorate. Where there are no effective Tories there can be no proper Whigs. As the struggle for power ceased to be political it became personal, a scuffle of the rival 'great houses' for the power to distribute the good things of Church and State.

In his autobiography, Trevelyan returned to this history of the subject:

While the principles of a single party united the Cabinet as a homogeneous body, capable of common action, the divergent principles of two parties divided Parliament into supporters of government and adherents of opposition. Thereby was secured steady support and steady criticism of the executive power, instead of irresponsible action prompted by the selfish impulses of individual members, or the mob psychology of undisciplined assemblies.

The two party system, the most convenient for the cabinet form of government, as Balfour observed, works only if there is a sufficient political difference between the two such that "a change of Administration would in fact be a revolution disguised under a constitutional change." Balfour described politics as "a game played between opponents who call themselves by different names but, so far as the average elector can see, do very much the same kind of thing in very much the same kind of way whenever they have the chance."[11]

A political party is a body of people who unite to advance a political cause (whether they understand the cause, is an other question). These people are ready to wave the banner of the *Common Good*. The political party system provides a way for a full airing of the questions effecting the public. The motivation to join political parties, at least those at the center and for those who have come into power, does not usually arise because of a particular belief which is passionately held. Sir James Fitzjames Stephen, lawyer, professor and judge:

All religions [movements] whatever, the professors of which aspire to rule mankind, have the same problem to grapple with. Each has an ideal of human nature to which its professors wish mankind in general to conform, or which they wish them, at all events, to admit to be entitled to reverence, whether they conform to it or not. Each of these religions finds a number of earnest and disinterested supporters, who are so much struck with its moral beauty and its inherent essential attractions that they become converts to it ... The loving, trusting, believing spirit wants neither reward nor punishment. He falls in love with his creed as a man might fall in love with a woman, without hope, but beyond the possibility of recovery. Persons like these are the core and heart of every great religion.

They form, however, a very small minority of the human race. The great mass of men is not capable of this kind of disinterested passion for anything whatever. On the other hand, they are open to offers. They can be threatened or bribed into more or less nominal adherence to almost any creed which does not demand too much of them.

Those with a passionate belief in a cause do *not* join a political party, they join with others who espouse the same cause, they become a member (more often informal than formal) of an "interest group."

Interest Groups:

While people in a democracy may well categorize themselves as being politically free, they inevitably suffer socially from that subtle and searching oppression which the dominant opinion of a free community may exercise over the members who compose it. Increasingly, however, the oppression is not so subtle. We are all exposed to the dupery of the cunning of people, as the British law reformer and judge, Henry Brougham expressed it, "who don't reflect," "who go about earewigging the powerful ones for their own purposes." The harm of elitist minorities whose goal it is to coerce the dispersed majorities for preferment was recognized earlier on by James Madison when he and others were framing up the constitution of that then fledgling country, the United States:

By a faction, understand a number of citizens, whether amounting to a majority or minority of the whole, who are united and actuated by some common impulse of passion, or of interest, adverse to the rights of other citizens, or to the permanent and aggregate interests of the community. ... A zeal for different opinions concerning religion, concerning government, and many other points, as well of speculation as of practice; an attachment of different leaders ambitiously contending for pre-eminence and power; or to persons of other descriptions whose fortunes have been interesting to the human passions, have, in turn, divided mankind into parties, inflamed them with mutual animosity, and rendered them much more disposed to vex and oppress each other than to cooperate for their common good. But the most common and durable source of factions has been the various and unequal distribution of property. ... To secure the public good, and private rights, against the danger of faction, and at the same time to preserve the spirit and form of popular government, is then the great object to which our inquiries are directed.   — *The Federalist Papers*, 1787.

Madison's plumed point, "To secure the public good, and private rights, against the danger of faction, and at the same time to preserve the spirit and form of popular government," is as valid today as when it was made better than two hundred years ago. The danger, because of the slick communications of the new age, is much more acute than it has ever been before. We are to pity the politician who should offend an interest group, for, next he goes to the polls to keep his seat, there will be a committee at the ready who will make every effort to turn the scales against him. This dependence, this "vote motive," as Bagehot was to observe, "weakens the intellectual influence of Parliament, and of that higher kind of mind of which Parliament ought to be the organ." (*Biographical Studies*.) More than ever, now, we see that the "vote motive" is a serious defect in a democratic political system. There is a tendency for each individual group to try to get its own way at the expense of the larger community. The "vote motive" promotes the formation of interest groups who attack, not one another, but, the public at large. Each seek to secure power, directly or indirectly, whereby the group would bind 100% of the citizens over into their ideas (legislation).

Democracy, the theme of it can never wear trite, is called a democracy because it looks to the interest, not of the few, but of the many. It is the sacred duty of those in an elected assembly, owed to the whole of the population, not to give in to any one of its parts for the sole benefit of that part. This is to be, no matter how meritorious the cause of that part, as for example, the "rights" of women, or "rights" of aboriginals. There is, unfortunately, however, an inherent tendency of myopic politicians to yield to the organized at the expense of the unorganized.

Any decision of any assembly must be in favor of its constituency, being those people who brought it into being by the electorial process. A government that is confused about its mandate in this regard falls under the sway of special interest groups.

When politicians fail, usually through sheer ignorance, of seeing to their most important duty as outlined in the previous paragraph, it becomes the duty of the citizenry to put up a howl. Do we howl when politicians shirk their solemn democratic role, hardly. Indeed, great numbers of us are enlisted by an exaggerated insistence upon the claims of sentiment, in the cause of some particular interest group, notwithstanding, that to sign on to this or that cause is to the very great disadvantage of themselves. Consumers versus producers — and this is a classic statement in political "science" — never seem to recognize their collective interests, or, at least, are seemingly unable to put up a common front against that which is plainly going to work against their larger interests. I quote the eminent economist, Arthur Seldon:

> The task is not easy because we all see our producer interest more vividly than our consumer interest. The rewards we can reap by prevailing on government to yield to our request or importunities or demands for 'help' are larger than the immediate losses we suffer as consumers. When farmers, coalminers, teachers, nurses, railwaymen, university professors, polytechnic teachers or government officials ask for and obtain larger subsidies, higher pay, shorter hours, longer holidays or better conditions than they are worth because it is politically expedient to keep them quiet, they gain as producers but lose as consumers in higher taxes or higher prices. But their gain is immediate, apparent and sizeable; their loss is distant, obscure and minuscule.
>
> The results are damaging to democracy. Since the cost of pressurizing government yields a much larger return in producer gains than it imposes in consumer losses, we tend to organize as

producers rather than as consumers. But in the end we all lose far more as consumers than we gain as producers: old industries, firms and occupations are kept alive, government is aggrandized, taxes are inflated, the articulate are incited to organize, the citizen is impelled to take to the streets to gain a hearing, parliament is bypassed.

Politicians:

Have you heard that politicians always take the required long-term view; that they always sacrifice their short-term political prospects; that they are always faithful to their promises of serving the public interest; that they put themselves last after all others; that they dissolve their empires, and withdraw to their homes and innocent pursuits when they can see that they are doing harm — if so, you have heard a gigantic fairy tale.

The image of the politician, very much earned through the years, I am afraid, is that of a sinister person, a shrewd schemer, a crafty plotter, an intriguer. A politician, as a general proposition, is a person who is keenly interested in politics; one who engages in party politics, or in political strife; and, above all, one who lives by politics as a trade. What he should be — and such persons have popped up in history, especially in the early years of the United States and throughout the 19th century in England — is an individual versed in the theory or science of government and the art of governing. He should be skilled in politics and is practically engaged in conducting the business of the state. He is to be, above all things, a statesman who knows very well that what he does will have a great effect on the welfare of the people of his country. What we are fixed with in these years are not statesmen, but rather politicians as first described, whose councils are directed by the momentary fluctuations of affairs.

Not that these politicians are unimpressive people. Most of them, especially those that get themselves elected time and time again, are quite impressive.[12] Usually, they impress people by their oratorical ability. However, one should not believe that there is a correlation between the degree of one's ability to speak in public, and say, to think or to deal with matters in an honest manner. Indeed, in regards to plain honesty, there is an indirect correlation. It's the slick talkers we need to watch out for. Effrontery and falsehood is all too often enough to defeat the side that is in the right. A clear and unprejudiced point of view founded on fact, sad to say, as is commonly observed, gives way to the crafty or fraudulent devices of the orator. The politician is not normally out to get at the truth of the matter, but rather to get an advantage, if not for himself directly then for the party. His object is to raise passion to such a level that it swamps reason. Then, at the moment the crowd reaches it highest point get them committed to a course of action.

The orator may wish to gain a special vote, to secure suffrages or to evoke from his hearers repeated confirmations of the policy he defends, and so to produce a modification of public opinion; but in any case his efforts are meant to rouse actual political action on the part of other people. His intention is to make others subserve his own ends, to strengthen his own scanty forces by means of the power that others possess, and this, whatever the character of his efforts, be they selfish or unselfish, be they directed to securing, the advantage of an individual, of a party, or of the state. A political speech is distinguished from a pamphlet, from expert advice, from a memorial or a dissertation, by the special fact that it seeks to bring about a comparatively rapid result, and to prevent a close and detailed examination of the subject under discussion. Vigorous, attractive, and even sweeping language, followed by a decision as rapid as possible before the flame of enthusiasm dies away, such is the course of events invariably most desirable to the great orator ...

A crowd of people is in most cases disinclined, and little competent to undertake, an accurate examination of the questions at issue, and the more incompetent it is the greater will be the influence exerted upon it but clever oratory. Where the influence of oratory is supreme we have to suppose a general decay of intellectual force ...

— Von Ruville.

That the mesmerized will stay mesmerized long after the mesmerizer has left their presence and that they will often then feel any injury that is inflicted on the mesmerizer — is a phenomenon which is worth a study. What is it in these men, in the their mode of oratory that extends their influence beyond the moment, beyond the occasion, beyond the immediate power shown. If one objectively listens to it, there is little in the average political speech that is remarkable or worth preserving. Is there anything at all that implies a habit of deep and refined reflection? What little knowledge one might gain from the politician in full oratorical flight is of the kind that lies within the reach of most of us with the expenditure of very little effort. The magic of oratory as William Hazlitt described, is due "to the powers of language, the chief miracle is, that a source of words so apt, forcible and well-arranged, so copious and unfailing, should have been found constantly open to express their ideas without any previous preparation." At least that is the way it seemed to Hazlitt. He continued:

They do not, it is true, allow of preparation at the moment, but they have the preparation of the preceding night, and of the night before that, and of nights, weeks, months and years of the same endless drudgery and routine, in going over the same subjects, argued (with some paltry difference) on the same grounds. Practice makes perfect. He who has got a speech by heart on any particular occasion, cannot be much gravelled for lack of matter on any similar occasion in future. Not only are the topics the same; the very same phrases — whole batches of them — are served up as the Order of the Day; the same parliamentary bead-roll of grave impertinence is twanged off, in full cadence by the Honourable Member or his Learned and Honourable Friend; and the well-known, voluminous, calculable periods roll over the drowsy ears of the auditors, almost before they are delivered from the vapid tongue that utters them! It may appear, at first sight, that here are a number of persons got together, picked out from the whole nation, who can speak at all times upon all subjects in the most exemplary manner; but the fact is, they only repeat the same things over and over on the same subjects — and they obtain credit for general capacity and ready wit, like Chaucer's Monk, who, by having three words of Latin always in his mouth, passed for a great scholar.

> — "On the Difference Between Writing and Speaking."

We do not need great scholars to run the affairs of government or do we need (as if such people existed) those who have all the answers. What is wanted are honest people who understand that progress, since the times of Newton, is made by the application of scientific principles.

Sir Karl Popper:

... what is needed most is the adoption of a critical attitude, and the realization that not only trial but also error is necessary. And he must learn not only to expect mistakes, but consciously to search for them. We all have an unscientific weakness for being always in the right, and this weakness seems to be particularly common among professional and amateur politicians. But the only way to apply something like scientific method in politics is to proceed on the assumption that there can be no political move which has no drawbacks, no undesirable consequences. To look out for these mistakes, to find them, to bring them into the open, to analyse them, and to learn from them, this is what a scientific politician as well as a political scientist must do. Scientific method in politics means that the great art of convincing ourselves that we have not made any mistakes, of ignoring them, of hiding them, and of blaming others for them, is replaced by the greater art of accepting the responsibility

for them, of trying to learn from them, and of applying this knowledge so that we may avoid them in the future
— *The Poverty of Historicism.*

Popper proceeds to point out on how our elected political representatives must proceed slowly and little by little. The reason for so proceeding is so that — and by the very definition of science (trial and error) mistakes will be made — the mistakes will be little ones. There is a correlation between the bigness of the trial and the bigness of the error. It is very hard to learn from very big mistakes. The reasons for this are twofold. First, given that large mistakes come from large enterprises, there can be no manageable feedback. Second, free discussion for all effected (the electorate) on large undertakings can hardly be tolerated if the plan is to go ahead at all. As Popper observed, "Accordingly there will always be a tendency to oppose the plan, and to complain about it. To many of these complaints the Utopian engineer will have to turn a deaf ear if he wishes to get anywhere at all; in fact, it will be part of his business to suppress unreasonable objections." And, remember, without feedback, there can be no scientific progress.

The process to which I have just referred is essentially one of learning and growing, of submitting our expectations to the test of experience, the control and correction of speculations. This is a process which is to be employed in evaluating what is the next best step for anyone of us to take as we proceed to deal with the endeavours of life. It is, since the welfare of a multitude of lives are at stake, particularly important for politicians who govern our country to employ such a process. But they seem not to know of it; their education, it certainly would appear, is sadly lacking. The typical politician appeals to the passions and prejudices of the crowd in order to simply obtain power. Whether it is by the methods of their pursuit or because they are so from the beginning (which drives them to be politicians in the first place) politicians have an overweening opinion of themselves, an overestimation of their own qualities, and a personal vanity or pride that seems to go along with most who posses magisterial power.[13] Sobering thoughts for them would be — politicians are not a race apart; they arise from the population; they are like the rest of us. Though there be exceptions, especially as history will show at times of national emergency, politicians are not better than the average sort of person. They are as a class not more able, not more kinder, not more moral, not less corruptible. A politician in power need only the normal set of virtues and to understand that for success in this life (this applies to all of us in any pursuit), we all need to rely on the goodwill of men and goodwill will be forthcoming to those who conduct themselves in keeping with the common principles of morality, that, in all of our dealings with others, to apply standards of right conduct and to avoid any form of wrong-doing or vice.

The first object and principle of action for every one of us is to do what is right; this is particularly so for politicians. And I have no doubt that politicians aim to do what is right, but more often than not they proceed to do what others think is right. The typical politician is forever "anxious to do all the good he can without hurting himself or his fair fame. His conscience and character compound matters very amicably. He rather patronises honesty than is a martyr to it. ... [He] has the pride of being familiar with the great, the vanity of being popular, the conceit of an approving conscience." Hazlitt continued to state that such a politician (in this case he was describing Lord Wilberforce) is not necessarily a hypocrite, as a hypocrite "is one who is the very reverse of, or who despises the character he pretends to be."

> He took it in a very cool and leisurely manner, watched his competitors with a wary, sarcastic eye, picked up the mistakes or absurdities that fell from them, and retorted them on their heads: told a story to the mob; and smiled and took snuff with a gentlemanly and becoming air, as if he was already seated in the House.
>
> — "Mr. Horne Tooke."

I would like to leave off on a positive note, like that earlier struck. All men, in the final analysis, in knowing what is good for them in their dealings with others proceed to do what is right and to avoid wrong-doing. One would think that of all the callings, those who seek political leadership would unfailingly follow the right road, the honest path. "Alas, both for the deed and for the cause!" One need but scan the pages of our newspapers, any week, and see how our politicians perform. The fact is that political power comes to those who persuade an efficient minority to coerce an indifferent and self-indulgent majority. Voting is but a promiscuous free-for-all scrimmage. In a democracy the people can be bribed, cajoled and bamboozled. The people's representatives in their pursuits are dishonest; and the people victimized by their own ignorance.

———————

"The Siren's Song."

> Man is the only animal that laughs and weeps; for he is the only animal that is struck with the difference between what things are, and what they ought to be. — William Hazlitt.

Liberalism:

Liberalism had its origins in the 19th century. It stood for liberty, both individual and national, with as little government as possible. It was a reaction to the aristocratic masters of those times when social privilege and authority were thought to be inheritable rights. Historically, liberals were of the view that there should be limits on social authority. Their creed was that there existed a private sphere of beliefs and conduct over which the individual should exercise autonomy. As the 19th century progressed the old aristocratic system was worn down, and while it was hoped that this power would be passed over to the people: it was not, and by and large, has not.

There are those today who flatter themselves by calling themselves "liberals." They are but socialists.[1] The socialist proceeds on the assumption that all concerned will judge rightly and act fairly — will think as they ought to think, and act as they ought to act; and these socialists assume this regardless of the daily experiences which we all have and which show that men do not necessarily act in such a fashion. These socialists, with their complaints that they make against the existing system, show their belief to be, that men have neither the wisdom nor the rectitude required by their plan, at least not under the principles of freedom and democracy. The utterances of socialists, as the Spanish philosopher, George Santayana wrote, is but "the babble of dreamers who walk through one world mentally beholding another." Liking them to flowers, Santayana wrote: "Their thoughts ... are all positings and deductions and asseverations of which ought to be, whilst the calm truth is marching unheeded outside."

We need but look at the history of the 20th century and see the damage and injury that has been brought on by those who proceeded to put into practice the theories of socialism. Attempts of establishing governments along socialistic lines, time and time again, have simply demonstrated its unworkability.[2] But, far worse, on every occasion, the outcome has been human misery. But, we hear yet, the Siren's Song of Socialism. Government action can create the good life for all. To begin with, government is not a neutral benevolent institution. But, let us forget and put aside the corrosive effect of Big Government — just, I hasten to add, for the purposes of this argument. It cannot be calculated what it is that people in society should do; and when, and how, and in what order it should be done. Society works because of the cooperation of people at the roots of society; it cannot be directed from the top by any form of government, one with good intentions or otherwise. Thankfully, for the coming into being of the human race and for its continuing maintenance, no knowing and directive force is required.[3] Things in nature organize themselves by nature not by reason; reason is but a mental process by which human beings sort out choices, a process which necessarily is limited by the number of choices a person can keep in mind — which, for most of us, is not too many at any one time.

We may achieve in our society, and not at general expense, full production and full distribution, and do so through the voluntary co-operation of most every one; intrusive and confiscatory government is not needed. There is a natural directive apparatus at work in this world which governs and supplies the needs and wants of human beings. There exists an egocentric mechanism which serves an extended order of collaboration. It is called the "market." Have you not marveled on how food is brought to your table; have you not wondered along the isles of a modern day grocery store and beheld the variety and cheap prices. It all comes to you, spontaneously, through a complex of interacting individuals or groups of individuals, all working consciously to advance themselves, and by so working, albeit unconsciously, advance society as a whole. It all comes about with very little social conflict simply in the desire of each person to gain a living by supplying the needs of his fellows. This marvellous system is fueled and driven by self-interest of the individuals within it.[4]

The simple and timeless fact, as described by Adam Smith in 1776, given the diversity of man's knowledge, only the individual, through his or her own industriousness and ingenuity, is capable of advancing his or her own particular interest or interests. It is only the individual person who can properly assess the matter before him or her, and considering what is at stake, it is that individual who knows how best to apply the needed industry and capital. It can only be the individual who has the matter at stake, who can best predict the product that might result from the application of his or her preserved industry and capital. It can only be the individual who can take into account his or her local situation, and being at the level where the action must take place, take the action which is likely required to achieve the desired results. No person can do these things for another even if they be described as a statesman or a lawgiver. If, the inappropriate, or wrong action is taken, or no action is taken where some was called for — with the result of an undesired impact on the individual, then that individual has no one to blame but himself or herself; and a lesson becomes available for the learning.

Philosophy:

We all take a great number of things for granted and many of these assumptions are of a philosophical character. We act on them in private life, in politics, in our work, and in every other sphere of our lives. It may be, that while some of these assumptions are true; some, I am obliged to point out, are just as likely false; and, indeed, harmful. Thus, as Popper[5] pointed out, we, each of us, have a moral duty to carry out a critical examination of our presuppositions, a philosophical activity.

Metaphysics is a philosophical area of study which concerns itself with the existence of things. Are things real? Or, do they exist simply in one's mind? Is the mind real? These are some of the elementary questions that come to one who inquires into the nature and ultimate significance of the universe. Those who hold reality subsists only in thought, are idealists (*idealism*); those who hold reality subsists in only matter, are realists or materialists (*materialism*); and those who hold that reality subsists in both in thought and in matter, are dualists (*dualism*).

Plato:

Plato, it may be concluded, was a dualist. In his work, the *Republic*, the putative wellspring of Western values, Plato sets forth his beliefs, among them being that there was another world beyond this changeable and destructible one in which we live, one consisting of unchanging eternal Forms. He asserted that what we see and touch are only very distantly related to the ultimate realities that exist. In addition, he believed that we are ineradicably social, and that the individual person was not, and could not, be self-sufficient. Plato took a dim view of democracy, thinking it absurd to give every person an equal say, since not every one is equally knowledgeable about what is best for society.

In Plato's scheme, private property was to be abolished, persons were not to own anything, "so that we can count on their being free from the dissentions that arise among men from the possession of property." (Incidentally, the people of Plato's *Republic* were to dump their children at central orphanages for the very same reason.)

But there is a dark and dreadful side to Plato. Plato's view of man is the same that one might have of a laboring beast of the field:

... And even in the smallest manner ... [one] should stand under leadership. For example, he should get up, or move, or wash, or take his meals ... only if he has been told to do so. In a word, he should teach his soul, by long habit, never to dream of acting independently ... There will be no end to the troubles of states, or of humanity itself, till philosophers become kings in this world, or til those we now call kings and rulers really and truly become philosophers, and political power and philosophy thus come into the same hands.

There was, in this world, to be no perfect state and no perfect men in it, one can only strive for the ideal. To Plato, there was no natural sense on how men ought to live, education was to be the key to the construction of a better society; from the "educated" would arise the elite to rule society. Plato thought it essential that a strict threefold class division be maintained. In addition to the rulers, the Philosopher-kings, there were to be "Auxiliaries" (soldiers, police and civil servants) and the "Workers" (the rest of us).

Plato's view of society was pinned by the belief that philosophers are capable of knowing the absolute truth about how to rule society, and, thus, are justified in wielding absolute power. Such a view is in striking contrast to that of Plato's principal teacher, Socrates, who was always conscious of how much he did not know, and claimed superiority to unthinking men only in that he was aware of his own ignorance, where they were not.

Descartes:

Any discussion of dualism would have to include reference to the French mathematician and philosopher, René Descartes (1596-1650). It was Descartes who formulated the axiom, *Cogito ergo sum*, "I think therefore I exist." Descartes was a dualist, viz. a man is of two natures, a spiritual nature and a temporal nature. Descartes, while he accepted some ideas were developed from experience, was steadfast in his belief that certain ideas were innate. By pure deduction Descartes evolved for himself entire universes that neither he, nor anyone else, could perceive by the use of their natural senses. All that was necessary for Descartes was intense self-examination and intense reason and through this process all would be revealed. The philosophy of a socialist whether he appreciates it, or not, is Cartesian; he or she is as steadfast as was Descartes in the belief that through pure reason humans can build a better world. Socialists are hardly ever discouraged by reality or are they much concerned with the true nature of man; theirs is a world they spin out of their heads, and, because they never in their schemes have to look beyond themselves, they have the pleasure of always being right.

Now, I think most every one would agree, a stable and efficient society is important; but one should wonder about a society that will use force (legislation) to make the individual give in to the desires of those who have set themselves up as knowing what is best for every one. Those who subscribe to such a theory, as we have seen, subscribe to Plato's theory of man. It is this theory upon which, in these times, our society rests. The theory is that the community is to permit government to use persuasion and force with a view to unite all citizens and make them share together the benefits which each individually can confer on the community for the benefit of the community. This theory, so attractive in its statement, is a false theory. When, in its legislation, in its use of force, government suppresses the welfare of the individual; when its efforts are aimed to foster the attitude that one should not proceed to please oneself, government commits a fatal error in the achievement of its laudable goal, the betterment of the whole. The essential problem in proceeding in this manner is that individuals cannot contribute to the whole, indeed will be a drain on the whole, unless they are allowed to be free and productive, that is to say allowed to suit themselves. Men did not evolve into robots; they did not come to possess the independent spirit, so characteristic of man, by serving others; man came to be the superior being — that he clearly is — because of the exercise of free choice, free choice the essential ingredient in the evolutionary process.

Down through the ages many thinkers and writers took their cue from Plato and speculated on social reform; most of them come from relatively recent times. Humans came out of their Dark Ages and into their Renaissance during the middle part of the second millennium, but a few hundred years were yet to pass before they started to seriously address their political and social situations. The Romantic Period (as a defined period, it does not go much beyond the limits of 1800 and 1825) heralded an encompassing age which covered certainly all of the 19th century, and which in many ways is still with us. An age, as described by John Stuart Mill[6], which is characterized by people who have become "destitute of faith" and "terrified at skepticism."

Political Process and Democracy:

The Platonic social engineers[7] can be heard to say, "Be docile, bow to leadership, obey the law: it is all for the common good. If, people were to be left alone to go about their own business — well, you know, to do so, well — it will just bring about social ruin: people, you know, are incapable, immoral and ignorant." (Why is it, I wonder, that these same social engineers defend, so passionately, the right of these same people to vote. The word democracy has, in itself, a clear enough meaning; but what happens when one adds the word social to democracy; "social democracy." It is a label for a political party that espouses a "social state," but the social state they imagine can only be founded and continue to exist — if one will only give the matter a modicum of thought — if there exists control over people, undemocratic despotism, benevolent or otherwise. These social dreamers commit a semantic fraud: "we will preserve individual freedom by doing away with freedom.")

While the political process is the center-piece of socialism there is one halting problem — the political process does not work. The collectivists, while pointing to the financial obstacles existing in a capitalistic system, create in their collectivist system a whole host of "cultural obstacles."[8] Special interests — elitist minorities whose goal it is to coerce the dispersed majorities for preferment on arbitrary grounds — move in and the resulting situation is perpetual unrest. And if one should want to get in on the debate, as the Chief Justice of Ontario, Charles L. Dubin, has pointed out, then that person should be ready to be denounced: as a racist, as a misogynist, as a supremacist, as a imperialist, or, as a facist; or a combination of any of the above. "Their [the spokepersons for interest groups] purpose often is to inflame — not to inform; to provoke — not to educate; to hector — not to reason, and frequently they impute dishonorable motives to those with whom they disagree."[9]

Because of its tyranny, we cannot leave important questions to the political process, indeed the political process is to be avoided. And thus, we have yet another reason to keep the functions of government to a minimum.

Lessons of History:

So we see, due to its faulty philosophical basis, socialism cannot work. And where attempted, the experiment has always ended in a wreck. Just look to recent history, that is all one needs to do. Collectivism has never really advanced beyond theory. As a governing mechanization, aside from the disastrous communist states of the 20th century, it is not to be seen in all of history. There is a reason for this. Persons who have a true sense of human nature, would think it too daunting a task. Imagine bringing into being and seeing to their workings, social institutions which were to bring to all members of human society, regardless of their station or income making ability, all of their life's needs with (and here's the kicker) the option for each of not working for these needs.

When I suggest recent history, I mean one need not go back any further than the early part of the 19th century. Read through the years from the times of Owen[10] and New Lanark, down through and into the present century. One will read of the social experiments of Nazi Germany and of the communistic states of Russia and eastern Europe. The evil empires of the 20th century were built on the ideals of sincere people determined to change society for the better, but who were wrong in their view of the nature of man. These idealistic dreamers were in error to think they could convert their dreams to reality. These social experiments brought about human misery, mostly untold. We stand now on higher ground and can look back on the world-wide downfall of socialism and the destruction which it wrought. Simply put, there existed in the past, and yet today it seems, people who had an abiding faith that the nature of man was changeable. These people forget that the nature of man was forged in an evolutionary process which extended over millions of years. The nature of man is not changeable; we are obliged to work with man as he exists not as we wish him to be. We can now make a final analysis. The choice is, either: "Do this or I will make you" or, "Do this, or take the consequences." The choice is to compel people to do what some think is right; or, to allow people to do, under the confines of criminal law, what they think is right through a system of voluntary co-operation, by civil contract.

But still there are those who with bright eyed innocence insist the world be shaped to their visions. Though they be benevolent, very well intentioned, very grave, and very respectable — they are, however, amateurs. And they carry the hallmark of all amateurs; they refuse to put aside subjective preference; they refuse to employ the scientific method.[11] Socialists believe in a grand system that has only ever existed in their collectivist heads. The use of rational argument will not shake them loose; they become like Jesuits at the burning pole.

Poverty and Morals:

I mean, now, to address a great problem which has long occupied the minds of practical statesmen and popular philosophers. The conflict between the rich and the poor. The conflict between those who possess property and those who do not. It is a conflict as old as time.

But first, let me say, before we get started with this discussion, that it is necessary to keep separated in one's mind two different concepts: the economic problems of production and distribution of wealth, and the moral principles of right and wrong.

Now, the thing that is thrown in the face of anyone who prefers freedom over collectivism, is, that such a course (no state intervention) is cruel and uncaring for the disadvantaged and the poor. The truth lies in just the opposite direction. Collectivism, as is so easily demonstrated, is a recipe for crime, corruption and a plastered environment. And it is, while it lasts, a system, which, as a general proposition, sucks up our scarce resources to such a point that little is left for those, who the collectivists say, should receive our collective help. The collectivist system, as has been demonstrated, is but only a method by which we transfer resources from the disadvantaged and poor to those who expound on the virtues of a collectivist system.[12]

Aside from the fact that there is an unacceptable slippage and waste when the state plays Robin Hood, there is the moral question of whether we should, by law, be forced to give up our property in favor of our neighbor? This leads us to a discussion of one's moral duties.

The moral system, again a natural system which runs without intervention, is sustained by two opposite principles of attraction and repulsion. These principles working in the heart of a normal person (the vast majority of us) lead us to do things for our fellow man; such as to feed the hungry, shelter the homeless, care for the sick, and enlighten the ignorant. A moral duty springs from the heart of the observer and is personal to that observer and comes about as a result of his or her experience, tradition and/or culture. A legal duty, I should distinguish, is that which is imposed upon a person from the outside, by a person or group who has coercive power over the law abider. The breach of either a legal duty or a moral duty will bring forth a penalty. In the case of the moral duty, the proscription of the penalty comes from within the person, himself or herself, its breach, in normal people, will bring on a feeling of shame and the fear of disfavor which may flow from friends and/or family. A penalty or a punishment imposed from without and as is proscribed by the law is what compels a person to obey law.[13] As to moral duties: each man must be his own judge in each particular case as to whether and how and how far, he can or will perform them.

We can all agree on the ends, which might well be summed up in words, "Distributive Justice." A number of us might also agree that to each his own "Moral Desert." The fact with which we must all come to grips, is, that there is inequality in the world and it is neither determined by, nor reconciled with, any deliberate moral judgments.

Poverty, according to the *OED*, is the "condition of having little or no wealth or material possessions. It is a state of indigence, of destitution, of want; ... Having few, or no, material possessions; wanting means to procure the comforts, or the necessaries, of life; needy, indigent, destitute; ... so destitute as to be dependent upon gifts or allowances for subsistence." The *OED* continues and points out that such a concept of poverty can be expressed in "various degrees, from absolute want to straitened circumstances ..." As Malthus observed in 1798, "poverty is relative." Most all of us can feel, to one degree or another, the pangs of "poverty" as we look to our richer neighbor. Sure now, any one of us will be able to draw a line between those who just want more and those who are in straitened circumstances. Sure, anyone of us will have no problem drawing a line.

The lines of all those who care to draw them, will not, however, fall to the same spot on the continuum. These lines will be all over the place and never will we be able to eliminate feelings of indigence from the general population and much damage can be caused in the try.

Much of the analysis in respect to poverty applies equally well to the disabled or disadvantaged that exist amongst us. One of us will point to a neonate who needs hundreds of thousands of dollars worth of our help, both at its moment of birth and throughout its cerebral palsied life; and another of us will point to the child who did not have a full breakfast this morning. For myself, I believe in charity. I believe you and I ought to help the poor and disadvantaged, each to give to the person, and to the degree, as each of us might determine. On no account should we employ the coercive and corrosive authority of the state to achieve charitable objects, as the state cannot achieve such objects.[14]

Any examination of the state's role in relieving poverty will reveal, not only the impossibility of such a task, but will further reveal, that in its tinkering, the state can only exacerbate the condition and make more widespread the existence of the evil which it wishes to get at (known as "The Law of Unintended Consequences"). What will become obvious to any researcher is the harmful effects of state assistance on personal character. Handouts, it will be observed, weaken the will and the capacity of the individual to escape from their lower state within the economy. It has been argued (Seldon) that money is the only ultimate teacher of discrimination and judgment in learning to choose the objects and services required in everyday living and in developing self-respect in the rebuilding of character. "Free" state services, instead of leaving people to contend with the opportunities and challenges of life and thus obliging them to build their own list of choices, have simply deprived them of the occasions to exercise judgment between alternatives in education, medical care, housing and providing for their old age. The solution is not further increments of state-provided services that require no effort by those who are in the best position to know and to provide the kind of assistance needed for others or for themselves.

The people who will relieve the poor and disadvantaged in our society can only be those who have a real heart for the matter. Those who can best identify the situation are the very same as those who are best able to bring forth the cure. The people who are in the best position to know and to provide the kind of assistance needed by those in need are those who are in the group which makes up the needful person's *family*; which, in the wider since, is that group to whom that person is attached. It cannot be expected that we can collectively respond to the emotions and needs of a stranger. Only an emotionally dependant person, a family member, can respond to the emotions and needs of a fellow family member. It cannot be expected that the normal family interaction can exist in the extended order of the wider society. While it is the notion of give and take that governs in any relationship — either a family relationship or one that exists in the extended order — in a family relationship we rely more on the notion of trust, simply because we have the repeated experiences of dealing with a particular member who now turns looking for help. We will extend emotional credit to a family member (and that too has its limits) but rarely to a "stranger" in the extended order.

The idea of human cooperation, and that which exists in the family system and that which is found in the extended system, is better dealt with under the topic of economics. Let me, however, express just a couple of thoughts on this topic. First we go to a Chinese sage in the mold of Confucius, Mencius (372-289 BC):

"The path of duty lies in what is near, and man seeks for it in what is remote." And, "Benevolence, righteousness, propriety, and knowledge are not infused into us from without." The plain fact is — and the proof is all about us — a gratuitous system intended to boost the family has just the opposite effect in that it diminishes the sentiment of parental responsibility. To bring a child into the world is to incur a grave responsibility, and no action of the State should tend to obscure the fact. To relieve parents from the costs of bearing and raising children will most emphatically diminish their motives for forethought. When government extends its "help" to parents and thus relieves them of their role to nurture their own children, and does so with coercive legislation (and let me tell you all legislation is coercive), passed in the name of progress, then the center of gravity shifts in the moral world from the parent, to the State. This shift undermines the foundation of national life by the deterioration of the social unit we know as *family*. This of course may very well fit some people's idea (Platonic idea) of the way the world ought to be run, where parenting is to be one of the roles of the state.[15]

I should not think it necessary to argue the proposition, but inequality exists in both the "systems" that we have labelled capitalism and socialism. It's just that inequality is easier to modify in a capitalistic system (for example the introduction of a negative income tax system or an inheritance tax). In fact, socialism is inherently one which promotes inequality: "The articulate, adroit and literate 'political' people extract more than the inarticulate, maladroit and illiterate 'domestic' people from the schools, hospitals, transport and other socialized services ..."[16]

A free enterpriser is not against the delivery of food to the hungry, or education and good medical care to all. All that a free enterpriser argues is that there is a better way to achieve such laudable objectives. No inference or a conclusion (*Non Sequitur*) can be made in respect to any difference in the ends to be achieved because one advocates a different means. Almost invariably, and it's a shame, those who advocate state altruism see themselves as saints and anyone who differs from them as inhumane monsters. If one objects to a thing being done by government, it should not be concluded that the objection is that it should not be done at all. To disapprove of state education is not to oppose education. To oppose state-enforced equality, is not to say one is against equality. These propositions are as absurd as stating that one is against people eating bread because he or she is against the state raising wheat.

Though they do not mean to be, and while one can attribute to them high motives, socialists are enemies of society. These do-gooding and meddlesome people, often by appealing to some of our finest instincts, and too, to the insecurities deep within us all — cause mischievous results. We should not allow ourselves to be guided, or governed by the principle that we should mostly do what we think is for the good of the body of society; for the good of the whole; for the good of others.[17] The same mischievous results are reached when one preaches that the object of government is to bring the most good to the most number; what the preachers fail to understand is that there is no good to be had out of socialism, none at all. As Winston Churchill said, "socialism is the philosophy of failure, the creed of ignorance and the gospel of envy." He added: "The inherent vice of capitalism is the uneven distribution of blessings; whereas the inherent virtue of socialism is the even division of misery."

Our objective is clear. It does not take a brilliant mind, or long years of study to see what we must do. We must strive to increase the sum of private happiness of the members of society. It comes about, as I hope I have demonstrated, because of individual actions, individual actions which are guided both by moral and legal duties. It cannot come about through the actions of an extended group such as is government.

> The old idea of a powerful philosopher-king who would put into practice some carefully thought out plans was a fairy-tale invented in the interest of a land-owning aristocracy. The democratic equivalent of this fairy-tale is the superstition that enough people of good will may be persuaded by rational argument to take planned action. History shows that the social reality is quite different. The course of historical development is never shaped by theoretical constructions, however excellent... Under no circumstances could the outcome of rational planning become a stable structure; for the balance of forces is bound to change. All social engineering, no matter how much it prides itself on its realism and on its scientific character, is doomed to remain a Utopian dream.
>
> — Popper, *The Poverty of Historicism.*

The Law of Nature:

If we are to bring about change, we must do so in accordance with the laws of nature. Man has gone to the moon and back and he has done so step by step, with each step in accord with the law of nature. Can we not likewise build a great society. The difficulty is, that coming to grips with a collection of bits of inert matter (such as that which goes to make up a space ship which will bring us to the moon), is a far different proposition from that of coming to grips with a collection of human beings. One might predict the specific results when the laws of nature are brought to bear on, relatively speaking, stable matter; it's entirely different when applied to human beings, which, independently are a law onto themselves. We most certainly cannot predict what any individual might do under any particular set of circumstances, though general trends might be stated.[18] It is these general trends, as winds of old, that might assist the ship of state to move her towards her destination, whatever that may be.

How are we to get at and solve the large social problems faced? It is an open question. What can be said, is that these problems will not be solved through the operation of a central committee. At the best of times, and with the best of members, and only if it be a simple matter, is it possible to lend a directive hand.[19] In regard to economic matters, the missing material needed for the proper deliberations of the committee is a continuous stream of market data. Committees do not have this stream of data, nor do they have the means, even with the most sophisticated computers, to deal with it. Even if the billions of mystic levers and buttons revealed themselves, the committee wouldn't know which ones to pull and to push, when to do it or in what sequence, or with what results — it's an impossibility. The simple answer to those who have the conceit of thinking they can set up and run a centralized economy by committee, is: "You have no idea of what drives an economy; it is driven at the roots by people who know their own wants and needs; and who, each of them, the millions, have the wherewithal to satisfy themselves by planning, and working, and trading; and, more generally, by learning to accommodate, and to learn, and to get along with their fellow human beings: all of this, so that each might satisfy their own particular set of wants and needs." Laws impinge on the essential ingredient of progress and of civilization and to the extent that laws are necessary, they must be certain and applicable to all.

The ultimate price we pay for collectivism is that democracy is docked and liberty is lost; the law of the jungle creeps back in with the final result being that there appears more human misery than ever there was before the collectivists first set in motion there freedom crushing machinery.

The only argument of those who advance the cause of collectivism, is that the human species is fundamentally evil and they need to be controlled, else we will all go about greedily taking things from one another; be nasty to one another. It is in the nature of man — these faithless collectivists assert — to be thoughtless, greedy and cruel. If this be the reason for putting on the controls of collectivism, then the question must be asked. Who are going to be the controllers? Who are we to put in charge? And the answer is, the same evil and greedy men from whom the collectivists wish to save us.

I do not advocate sitting around and doing nothing, but likely all that is available to us is, as Sir Karl Popper put it, "social midwifery." None of what I have said should be construed as giving up the "systematic fight against definite wrongs, against concrete forms of injustice or exploitation, and unavoidable suffering such as poverty or unemployment;" but such a fight "is a very different thing from the attempt to realize a distant ideal blueprint of society." And always, we must be aware of "an accumulation of power, and to the suppression of criticism."

History, particularly of the earlier ages, will tell of the growth and maintenance of our customs and traditions. History of the last two hundred years, however, will show the deterioration of customs and traditions that took a long, long time to develop. It will show that this deterioration came about on account of man's meddlesome ways and in his interference with a natural process in attempting to impose his rationalistic views on the suitability of customs and traditions. These attempts have done nothing but impede, or reverse the process of man's cultural development, and have brought about untold burdens of human misery.

We must fear those who demand the use of force in order to substitute their own inclinations for those of the human race. We must fear those who desire to set themselves above mankind in order to arrange, organize, and regulate it according to their fancy. We must fear those who think only of subjecting mankind to the philanthropic tyranny of their own socialistic inventions. We must fear those who desire to force mankind docilely to bear a yoke of the public welfare. We must fear those who proceed, always, on this triple hypothesis: the total inertness of mankind, the omnipotence of the law, and the infallibility of the legislature.

———————————

Notes

Notes for "On Liberty."

1   *N.Y. Times* 7 Jan. 4/7.

2   Normal people in normal circumstances act through passion and tradition, more than through rational thought. Thus it is very important when addressing social issues that the role of tradition, culture and family be given careful consideration.

3   A Concept, according to the *OED*, is a thought, or an idea. "The product of the faculty of conception .... concepts are merely the results, rendered permanent by language, of a previous process of comparison ... a concept is a general representation of a whole class of things." This definition of concept is to be compared with the word, percept, which, on my understanding, are the mental bits or parts (percepts) which cannot be conceived by the brain but from which the brain forms a concept, or a thought or an idea which may or may not invoke, through a further mental process, the body's muscles to take action. A percept is to be distinguished from the action. As one of the editors of the *OED* observed, it was William James who sometimes used the word percept to refer to "the content of consciousness during perception." Technically, then, a percept is a particular pathway that leads from the senses of the being, such as the sense of sight, where, "the visual image formed on the retina by light rays entering the eye is transformed into a visual percept, on the basis of which appropriate commands to the muscles are issued." And further, "each physical stimulus, after interpretation by the mental processes, will result in a percept."

4   The demarcation of classes of people — groups within society, groups with differing ranks and privileges — may be lines determined by birth (certainly that was the case in earlier ages), or by wealth, or by force, or by those employed or not employed by government. As for economics: while the complex, the social structure, is large and can be made to appear complicated by the incalculable actions of all the self-directed individuals working within it, the economy is run, nonetheless, by a rather simple set of laws. I say parenthetically that the subject of economics unfortunately has been made out to be complicated by people, who claim to be in the know. These economists, these

prognosticators with their pointy hats and crystal balls, have been employed by politicians so to justified the free spending ways of big government.

5   For a concrete example, let me turn to a piece of federal legislation, *Employment Equity Act*. Section 4 of that act, so I read, requires employment policies of those with federal contracts of over $100,000 to be based on race, sex, ancestry, appearance or disability, the numbers depending on the percentage of the traits in the population. Under such a regime we can be sure, from the lowly filing clerk to the supreme court judge, the best will not be had and those chosen can never assert with pride to themselves or others that they got to their position on their "own merits." At the very least, pride of position is tarnished. Worse yet, those massive numbers not chosen will be unhappy with their "achieved" level and frustrated with the feeling that they cannot personally advance themselves.

Notes for "The Law."

1   "Laws are like cobwebs, which may catch small flies, but let wasps and hornets break through." (Swift, 1709.)

2   It was the French philosopher and jurist, Montesquieu (1689-1755) who said, "The spread of civilization and sweet manners to the barbarians came about as a result of commerce."

3   I mark the words the state could be a rational instrument "in bringing peace" to society. For those unacquainted with the history of the last two hundred years, all the scientific observations are that man is best left, under appropriate criminal law, to govern himself. As the philosopher Karl Popper did, we might liken "social science" to "midwifery." It is the mother not the midwife who is obliged to go through the untidy and the painful business of delivering her baby. So it is, not only can a state not be run by a controlling mind, but, as the Roman statesman Cicero pointed out, the controlling mechanisms cannot even be set by one controlling mind (much less by a committee). A lasting state can only evolve through the passing of several generations, viz. it comes into being only after the passage of a considerable period of time. "Our state, ..." as Cicero wrote fifty years before the birth of Christ, "Our state, on the contrary, is not due to the personal creation of one man, but of very many;

it has not been founded during the lifetime of any particular individual, but through a series of centuries and generations. There never was in the world a man so clever as to foresee everything and that even if we could concentrate all brains into the head of one man, it would be impossible for him to provide for everything at one time without having the experience that comes from practice through a long period of history." (Leoni.)

4 "My designe being not to shew what is Law here, and there, but what is Law." (Hobbes.)

5 As Jonathan Swift wrote in 1724, "In all free nations I take the proper definition of law to be, The will of the majority of those who have the property in land."

6 It is my view that most politicians are demagogues. Their sole aim in life is to get and keep political power, and do so by catering to the noisy interest groups who are out to gratify themselves at the expense of the whole. "A plausible, insignificant word, in the mouth of an expert demagogue, is a dangerous and a dreadful weapon." (Robert South, 1634-1716, a stout Royalist.) "... oft the cheated crowd adore The thriving knaves that keep them poor." (Gay: *Fables*.)

7 It was in his work, *The Principles of Morals and Legislation* that Bentham made the "scientific attempt to assess the moral content of human action by focusing on its results or consequences."

8 The common law is an immeasurable set of laws, or rather as Bagehot expressed it, "they are declarations of immemorial custom, not precepts of new duties." Common law is what Englishmen have relied upon for hundreds of years, and led them for a period of time to be the masters of the world. It still exists in countries which can point to a British heritage such as that of Canada and of the United States.

9 This is unlike the theories of Plato and Aristotle. Plato and Aristotle taught that governments came about because there exists a social instinct in man to gather together under powerful councils, i.e., it was natural for man to put himself under government.

10 Man is collectivist. Intensively so at the family level, less so at the tribe level, hardly at all at larger levels.

11 Justice Benjamin Nathan Cardozo (1870-1938) who was appointed to the United States Supreme Court in 1932, was an eloquent

and influential supporter of liberal social and economic views. His published lectures are considered classics of jurisprudence.

Notes for "The Common Law."

1   The scientific method is the inductive reasoning process strictly applied. The scientific method demands that all assumptions be questioned, it is skeptical to a degree, and starts with the fundamental assumption that material effect is impossible without material cause. Scientific theories, and this is just as so for philosophic statements, can only be put as hypotheses, propositions, which can never be known as certain, but which can be deliberately put to the test of observation and experiment, and revised or rejected if their predictions get falsified. (See Popper's work.)

Notes for "On Legislation."

1   Malthus laid down four rules. These rules, incidentally, may be broadly applied to any course of action. Terms, Malthus points out, must be carefully defined before their use. An agreement must be worked out on the meaning of the terms used and it should, as closely as possible, correspond with the sense understood in the ordinary use of them. Secondly, where no agreement on meaning can be reached, in order to continue the discussion, the meaning to be taken is that which "the most celebrated writers" have accepted and used. In this process the parties should not "be bound down by past authority" and a change might be introduced "whenever it can be clearly made out that a change would be beneficial, and decidedly contribute to the advancement of the science." However, Malthus cautioned: "if we determine to have a new one in every case where the old one is not quite complete, the chances are, that we shall subject the science to all the very serious disadvantages of a frequent change of terms, without finally accomplishing our object." Thirdly, the project (legislation) proposed should not only remove the immediate objections (the social evils to be got at) but should be shown to be free from other or greater objections, though a "change which is always itself an evil, can alone be warranted by superior utility taken in the most enlarged sense." Fourthly, "any new definitions adopted should be consistent

with those which are allowed to remain ..." Of course, as Malthus pointed out, in the application of the rules, we must always keep in view the object under consideration.

2   The socialist movement was driven, in England, in the 1930s, by the Fabian writings of the "Bloomsbury Group" which centered around Cambridge and included such literary lights as Malcolm Muggeridge, Beatrice and Sidney Webb, Geo. Bernard Shaw, H. G. Wells, Virginia Woolf, and, of course, John Maynard Keynes. I cannot help myself, I editorialize. Socialists always proceed on this triple hypothesis: the total inertness of mankind, the omnipotence of the law, and the infallibility of the legislature. There is, I surmise, a disproportionate number of "educated" people who are socialists, people who may or may not have drunk deep enough from the Pierian spring; but who, at any rate, certainly have their heads down feeding in the socialistic troughs, which government fills with our money. The light of their grand objectives blinds them, as well as us. "Socialists (of varying kinds) believe in socialism (of varying kinds); they are generally unapologetic; they are industrious writers, lecturers, persuaders, activists, organizers and conference-goers, movers of motions and dealers in doctrines." (Seldon.)

3   No matter which legislative scheme you might want to examine, I submit, on the whole, we are no better off; most of our social ills continue, and new ones have arrived which are of a much more virulent kind. And through it all our liberties have suffered with burgeoned bureaucracies and our economy (a fixed system by which the life blood of society flows) has been deaden by huge and unmanageable government debt.

4   Judges and legislators are very touchy about the expression "judge made law"; it is against Montesquian doctrine for judges to make laws. Judges cut and skin the law here and there, but they no more make laws than lumbermen make logs. Though a judge on occasion may cross the line, a vigorous lawyer and an appeal court will soon cure it. The standard psychological attitude for a judge is to "discover" the law, not to "create" it.

5   "If every person has the right to defend — even by force — his person, his liberty, and his property, then it follows that a group of men have the right to organize and support a common force to protect these rights constantly. This principle of collective right — its reason for existing, its lawfulness — is based on individual

right. And the common force that protects this collective right cannot logically have any other purpose or any other mission than that for which it acts as a substitute. Thus, since an individual cannot lawfully use force against the person, liberty, or property of another individual, then the common force — for the same reason — cannot lawfully be used to destroy the person, liberty, or property of individuals or groups." (Bastiat, *The Law*, 1850.)

6   A moral belief is held (tenent) because it has been found, through experience — whether people are particularly conscious of the process, or not — that it works. When the practice dictated by the moral belief starts to not bring the expected and desired results, then, in a relatively short period, the moral belief turns into a pure superstition and the practice changes.

Notes for "On Property Rights."

1   Sumner, who taught at Yale at the turn of the 20th century, continues, "it is, therefore, the hardest to understand, the most delicate to meddle with, and the easiest to dogmatize about."

2   The sun and the rain are common to all men. This only because they cannot be possessed, or excluded, or improved upon.

3   "Few enjoyments are given us from the open and liberal hand of nature; but by art, labor and industry we can extract them in great abundance. Hence the ideas of property became necessary in all civil society." (Hume's *Enquiry*.)

4   As a wise judge once said, and I forget who, "It should be remembered that of the three fundamental principles which underlie government, and for which government exists, the protection of life, liberty and property, the chief of these is property; not that any amount of property is more valuable than the life or liberty of the citizen, but the history of civilization proves that, when the citizen is deprived of the free use and enjoyment of his property, anarchy and revolution follow, and life and liberty are without protection."

5   Emerson compared the creation of wealth to the falling of snow, "if snow fall level today, it will be blown into drifts tomorrow." (*Nature*, 1836.) It is, unquestionably, one of the great functions of government, to continue this metaphor, to get some strategically placed snow fences in place; but it

is impossible for it to call for the right snowfall and the right winds, or to bulldoze it off of one field and onto another.

6   The socialist grounds his argument for state control on the Hobbesian notion that man is fundamentally corrupt (cf. John Locke's theory). And, yet, the socialist "proceeds on the assumption that all concerned will judge rightly and act fairly — will think as they ought to think, and act as they ought to act; and he assumes this regardless of the daily experiences which show him that men do neither the one nor the other, and forgetting that the complaints he makes against the existing system show his belief to be that men have neither the wisdom nor the rectitude which his plan requires them to have." (Herbert Spencer.)

7   "The instinct of ownership is fundamental in man's nature." (William James.)

8   It was to be the middle of the 19th century before the theories of evolution (theories supported by hard facts) were to be discussed and accepted; Locke's views are consistent with evolution. That which distinguishes man from the animals is man's capacity to communicate and cooperate with one another, a capacity which evolved slowly over millions of years and which could not possibly evolve in the "solitary and brutish" world which Hobbes thought existed.

9   The most important question for us all is, What is the nature of man? One's view of this will completely colour his life. Shelley in *Queen Mob* painted two views:

> Man is of soul and body, formed for deeds
> Of high resolve; on fancy's boldest wing
> To sour unwearied, freelessly to turn
> The keenest pangs to peacefulness, and taste
> The joys which mingled sense and spirit yield;
> Or he is formed for objectiveness and woe,
> To gravel on the dunghill of his fears,
> To shrink at every sound, ...

Neither one of Shelley's poetic views are correct. Man in his natural state was, in this writer's opinion, proud and full of "high resolve." He had to be to survive. Life for "primitive man" was objective. He had to be to survive. "Primitive man" could not long be carried away with mysticism, for him there was the reality of chasing down supper and hauling it back to his hard fought for and defended shelter. He hardly could afford "to gravel on the dunghill of his fears," or "to shrink at every sound." "Primitive man" was led, by his careful observations, to proper conclusions, or he died.

10   I should add that the idea that the right to property was a natural right, was not something newly asserted by Locke. It was a fundamental concept of the medieval church, one that was first proposed by Aristotle. The English constitutional principle as to the right of a person to possess and own property continues to be fully supported by the Roman catholic church as it came into the 20th century. "Every man has by nature the right to possess property of his own. This is one of the Chief points of distinction between man and the lower animals." (Pope Leo XIII, *Rerum novarum*, May 15th, 1891.) "The right to hold property is a natural right. It is the safeguard of family life, the stimulus and the reward for work." (*Pastoral Letter of the French Roman Catholic Hierarchy*, Spring, 1919.)

11   There are, of course, fruits of the earth that readily come to us with little or no labor, and often, as a result, have little or no value.

12   "The law does not say to a man, 'Work, and I will reward you;' but it says to him, 'Work, and by stopping the hand that would take them from you, I will insure to you the fruits of your labor, its natural and sufficient reward, which, without me, you could not preserve.' If industry creates, it is the law which preserves it, at the first moment, we owe everything to labour, at the second, and every succeeding moment, we owe everything to the law." (Bentham's *The Principles of the Civil Code*.)

13   Men, who have no moral ties to family or community, will resort to plunder whenever plunder is easier than work. Plunder usually will stop when it becomes more painful and more dangerous to acquire the sought after property than it is to expend the labor necessary to acquire it honestly. It is this reason that the law evolved to protect property and punish plunder. Of course, in a collectivist state, with nobody owning property then no one will be able to plunder another — and that's true; however, in a socialistic state, almost everybody will be too busy plundering the state, and, I might add, the state will be busy plundering its citizens to make up for its losses (the

whole set up soon collapses). How does it all come to this? It all starts out with the social engineers, the collectivists who from the start are driven by their Platonic ideas and the noble notion of governing people in a manner that will make them happier.

14 The right to hold property explicitly exists in the written constitution of the United States and it exists in the unwritten constitution of Canada. That it was not written down in the *Canadian Charter of 1982* should not give a moment's bother to a constitutional historian. The right to property is a constitutional right which has long existed in the English constitution, and the English constitution is one in which the Canadian constitution is firmly rooted. Further, it is to be noted, that The Constitution of 1774 (*The Quebec Act*) confirmed that people had a "constitution and system of laws, by which their persons and property had been protected," a provision which was specifically retained by section 26 of the 1982 *Charter*.

This is not a proposition which has been much appreciated by the Canadian courts. It seems, almost, that our judges have been proceeding on the basis that *The Canadian Charter of Rights* is the fountain-head of our constitutional rights. This is demonstratively not so. Justice Dickson, in his written decision in the *Irwin Toy* case (SSC,1989) is illustrative of the point. The Supreme Court of Canada was focused on the application on a particular group who were advancing the notion that people had a constitutional right to welfare. Dickson, J., wrote: "What is immediately striking about this section [s. 7 of *The Charter*] is the inclusion of 'security of the person' as opposed to 'property'. This stands in contrast to the classic liberal formulation, adopted, for example, in the Fifth and Fourteenth Amendments in the American Bill of Rights, which provide that no person shall be deprived 'of life, liberty or property, without due process of law'. The intentional exclusion of property from s. 7, and the substitution therefor of 'security of the person' has, in our estimation, a dual effect. First, it leads to a general inference that economic rights as generally encompassed by the term 'property' are not within the perimeters of the s. 7 guarantee. This is not to declare, however, that no right with an economic component can fall within 'security of the person.' ... We do not, at this moment, choose to pronounce upon whether those economic rights [the learned judge had given examples: rights to social security, equal pay for equal work, adequate food, clothing and shelter] fundamental to human life or survival are to be treated as though they are of the same ilk as corporate-commercial economic rights." That the Supreme Court of Canada seemingly has forgotten our constitutional roots is further seen by Lamer, J's. decision in the *Prostitution Reference* case (SSC, 1990): "... I pause to note that in applying principles developed under a provision of the U.S. Constitution to cases arising under our *Charter*, the court must take into account differences in wording and historical foundations of the two documents. (1166) ... I therefore reject the application of the American line of cases that suggest that liberty under the Fourteenth Amendment includes liberty of contract. As I stated earlier these cases have a specific historical context, a context that incorporated into the American jurisprudence certain *laissez-faire* principles that may not have a corresponding application to the interpretation of *The Charter* in the present day. ..." (1170.) This "history" to which Justice Lamer obliquely refers is the same history for both Canada and the United States. Lamer, J., continued and pointed out that the courts will not let section 7 get in the way of "the realm of general public policy dealing with broadly social, political and moral issues which are much better resolved in the political or legislative forum and not in the courts. ... It is important to note that the onus is on the person bringing the challenge to demonstrate not only the restriction of the rights but also that the state has not abided by the principles of fundamental justice." (1176.) And finally: "... it is desirable to maintain a conceptual distinction between the rights guaranteed by s. 7 and the other freedoms in *The Charter*." And with these pronouncements, it seems, important constitutional rights, which have taken hundreds of years to build up, were swept away.

Notes for "On Rights."

1   "Association, however, necessarily creates rights and duties; from rights and duties spring law and government." (Traill.)

2   Such as those found in the American Declaration of Independence (1776) — "life, liberty and the pursuit of happiness"; or as may be found in the *Canadian Charter* (1982) — "life, liberty and security of the person"; or as may be found in *The Universal*

Declaration of Human Rights as adopted in 1949 by the General Assembly of the United Nations: "That all men are by nature equally free and independent, and have certain inherent rights of which, when they enter into a state of society, they cannot ... deprive or divest their posterity; namely, the enjoyment of life and liberty, with the means of acquiring and possessing property, and pursuing and obtaining happiness and safety."

3   Indeed, freedom is an absolute necessity to life. Freedom is not something we have gained through the efforts of our ancestors. Rather it is something with which we are born; it comes with life's package. It is something that is necessary to our very evolvement and is necessary to our continued involvement in life.

4   Burke's admonishment comes to mind, "We are just on the verge of Darkness and one push drives us in." (As quoted by Kirk.)

5   In 1215, King John signed The Great Charter (*The Magna Carta*) in which is rooted the right to a jury trial and the right not to be deprived of liberty except by due process of law.

6   That a man cannot be compelled to give evidence against himself is traceable back to the *Petition of Right*, 1628.

7   The prohibition of excessive bail and of cruel or unusual punishments is traceable back to the *English Bill of Rights*, 1689.

8   It is, of course, a most difficult job and likely not one that could be completed — to list "the innumerable rights of an Englishman." In the Canadian listing, the *Charter* of 1982, one of the most essential rights, the right to possess property was omitted. Though omitted, property rights nonetheless exist; and, by virtue of section 26, are preserved: "The guarantee in this *Charter* of certain rights and freedoms shall not be construed as denying the existence of any other rights or freedoms that exist in Canada." Why such an obvious constitutional right was omitted from the listing was, I think, because the whole exercise was a study in compromise. There was then, and there is now, a faction ignorant of basic economics, as they indeed are, who believe that property is a dirty word. That property rights were omitted, was bad enough, but worse, and which made the whole event an exercise in futility, was the inclusion of section 33, which, in effect, allows the Parliament of Canada

or any of the provincial legislatures to declare that the listed rights in the *Charter* might be suspended. These Canadian politicians, by section 33, pretend to give themselves the ability to trample over the rights of Canadians. They do not have that ability; they never did have that ability; nor can they create it by fiat, by their legislation. They have made a joke out of Madison's notion that civil rights must be entrenched in a country's constitution so to be an "impenetrable bulwark."

Notes for "Criminal Law and The War on Drugs."

1   Hume in his *Enquiry* continued and observed that men, as objects of scientific study, have no more changed in the last two or three thousand years, than has any other object worthy of scientific study; the sun whirls about under the same laws, and men's behavour is just as predictable no matter what period of recorded time one may choose.
2   Cory J., *Knox Contracting*, 1990, S.C.C.
3   Blackstone defined "a crime, or misdemeanor, as an act committed, or omitted, in violation of a public law, either forbidding or commanding it." John Austin (1790-1859), compared it in contradistinction to a civil action (an offence pursued at the discretion of the injured party) as "an offence pursued by the Sovereign or by the subordinates of the Sovereign ..."
4   Such a study would begin with Sir Edward Coke's work, *Institutes of the Laws of England* (1628-44) and certainly include a review of Sir James Stephen's seminal work, *History of the Criminal Law* (1883).
5   Rand J., *The Margarine Reference*, 1949, S.C.C.
6   Rand J., *Goodyear Tire and Rubber*.
7   The American experience (and it cannot be much different here in Canada) will show how drug prohibition actually escalates violent crime. See, *The Economic Anatomy of a Drug War* by David W. Rasmussen and Bruce L. Benson.

Notes for "Crime and Punishment."

1   These lines are Daniel Defoe's, "Hymn to the Pillory," written just before, as a religious dissenter, in 1704, he was pilloried for the writing of the pamphlet, *The Shortest Way with the Dissenters*. In the next four lines, Defoe set out thoughts on the law:

"But justice is interverted, when
Those engines of the law,
Instead of pinching vicious men,
Keep honest ones in awe."

2   There are, assuming one cannot commit a crime against one's self, "victimless crimes," such as, suicide, drugs, prostitution, gambling, etc. Sir James Fitzjames Stephen — the principal drafter of the Criminal Code of Canada (1892), which, in many of its parts, still exist today — expressed the view that legislation ("the roughest engine which society can use for any purpose") is to be used to improve morals. This position is to be contrasted to that of the American jurist, Oliver Wendell Holmes who did not think that law ought to be used for this end, at all. By the way — Stephen was a Christian: Holmes, an atheist.

3   "An act punishable by law, as being forbidden by statute or injurious to the public welfare." (*OED*.) Or, as H.L. Mencken defined it: "society, in order to protect the weak and botched against the bold and original, has had to proclaim certain human acts, under certain circumstances, as too dangerous to be permitted." ("Crime and Punishment" as contained in the May, 1922 ed. of the *Smart Set*.)

4   "The conception of crime which the ordinary citizen entertains involves the commission of some act which transgresses not merely the law but morality. Murder, robbery, arson, perjury and the like all offend the natural instincts of the good citizen and their repression commands his assent. But in recent times the criminal law has invaded almost every department of daily life with countless restrictions to the contravention of which penal consequences are attached. People may now be arraigned for acts which are in no sense intrinsically wicked but are merely made crimes by an Act of Parliament in pursuance either of economic exigencies or political theories." (Lord MacMillan, in his introduction to Professor Leon Radzinowicz' work, *History of Criminal Law and Its Administration*.) The criteria in the passing of criminal laws — which by implication means ultimately the application of force by government against the citizen — has been significantly (and I think wrongly) altered from that simple criteria which was set forth many years ago by John Stuart Mill: "... the only purpose for which power can be

rightfully exercised over any member of a civilized community against his will is to prevent harm to others. His own good, either physical or moral, is not a sufficient warrant. He cannot rightfully be compelled to do or to forbear because it will be better for him to do so, because it will make him happier, because in the opinions of others to do so would be wise or even right. These are good reasons for remonstrating with him, or reasoning with him, or persuading him, or entreating him, but not for compelling him, or visiting him with any evil in case he do otherwise. To justify that, the conduct from which it is desired to deter him must be calculated to produce evil to someone else." (*On Liberty.*)

5   The Star Chamber is a synonym for arbitrary and oppressive administration of punitive justice. It is the appellation of an apartment in the royal palace at Westminster, in which during the 14th and the 15th century, the chancellor, treasurer, justices, and other members of the king's Council sat. They did not feel compelled to exercise their jurisdiction in any prescribed fashion, other than to achieve the ends of the crown. It is this history which led, very early, unlike the common law, to a legislative adoption "that there must be chapter and verse of the written law behind every punishment." (Roscoe Pound, in his introduction to Saleilles' work, *The Individualization of Punishment.*)

6   *The Canadian Charter of Rights*, for example, provide: s.2, "Every one has the following fundamental freedoms: (a) freedom of conscience and religion, (b) freedom of thought, belief, opinion and expression, including freedom of the press and other media of communication, (c) freedom of peaceful assembly; and (d) freedom of association"; s.7, "Every one has the right to life, liberty and security of the person and the right not to be deprived thereof except in accordance with the principles of fundamental justice"; s.8, "Every one has the right to be secure against unreasonable search or seizure"; s.10, "Every one has the right on arrest or detention, (a) to be informed promptly of the reasons therefor, (b) to retain and instruct counsel without delay and to be informed of that right, and (c) to have the validity of the detention determined by way of *habeas corpus* and to be released if the detention is not lawful"; s.11, "Any person charged with an offence has

the right (a) to be informed without unreasonable delay of the specific offence, (b) to be tried within a reasonable time, etc."

7   "We must, wherever we suppose a Law, suppose also some Reward or Punishment annexed to that Rule." (Locke's *Human Understanding*.) It is thought, and it seems reasonable enough, that, in "general, the method of punishment is more satisfactory than the method of reward, because it can be controlled to a greater extent." (R. M. Yerkes, as quoted by *OED*.)

8   *Lex talionis* are fancy Latin words meaning the law of equivalent retaliation, and which, for lawyers, has a legal meaning which extends into a whole system of laws, of which the *Code of Hammurabi*, the earliest code of laws known to history, is a perfect example. "In general the principle of punishment was the *lex talionis*: 'life for life, eye for eye, tooth for tooth, hand for hand, foot for foot, burning for burning, stripe for stripe' ... *The Mosaic Code*, though written down at least fifteen hundred years later, shows no advance, in criminal legislation, upon the *Code of Hammurabi*; in legal organization it shows an archaic retrogression to primitive ecclesiastical control." (Will Durant, *Our Oriental Heritage*.)

9   Fear is twofold; servile, whereby punishment, not fault, is dreaded; filial, by which fault is feared. It is this filial fear, or shame which has long been the sheet-anchor of the law. However, "Shame is no punishment except upon persons of ingenuous dispositions." [Joseph Priestley (1733-1804).]

10   Since 1892, legislators "were influenced to implement such reform in annual legislation, which introduced inconsistencies in the code and made it bulky and unwieldy. The restructuring of 1954 reduced the bulk and removed many of the inconsistencies as well as most of the anomalies incorporated by default or accident in the 1892 legislation. With the creation of the Law Reform Commission, a permanent organization was established which has been a fruitful source of ideas for progressive change in the criminal law, and has pointed the way to a new model code. ... The commissioners can ponder the law; they can conceive and draft programs of progressive reform; and they can put forward those programs for implementation by Parliament. But politicians march to a different drummer ..." [*The Genesis of the Canadian Criminal Code of 1892*.]

11   "The laws of the most kingdoms and states have been like buildings of many pieces, and patched up from time to time according to occasion, without frame or model. ... This continual heaping up of laws without digesting them maketh but a chaos and confusion, and turneth the laws many times to become but snares for the people. ... Then look into the state of your laws and justice of your land: purge out multiplicity of laws: clear the incertainty of them: repeal those that are snaring; and press the execution of those that are wholesome and necessary ..." These are the words of Francis Bacon written some 400 years back.

12   Lord MacMillan in his introduction to Radzinowicz' work. The arcanal and duplicative provisions need to be tossed. This could be done in a re-write. But, to eliminate victimless crimes, as for example those relating to prostitution, pornography, and drugs — is another matter. To obtain a consensus in respect to constructive laws is extremely difficult in a democracy, indeed, next to impossible.

13   The *Magna Carta* provided that mercy might be shown to villains, but only "by the oath of honest men of the vicinage." (Art. 20.)

14   There is nothing new about this. In part, this has been operating in our criminal law system for a considerable period of time. This approach has its roots in the law of outlawry. The notion of outlawry is timeless and maybe spotted in all societies of men. When a wrongdoer is brought before the ruling Council, a finding of guilt would mean he was turned loose to the victim, the victim's family, or, for that matter, anybody else who would like to join in; anything that the mob should inflict, from death to torture, was, OK. The maxim applicable to outlaws is, "Let them be answerable to all, and none to them." A person outlawed had no more rights than a dead man, *civiliter mortuus*. One, thus put outside the law, was deprived of its benefits and protection; one was then under a sentence of outlawry, a sentence, in times past that was worse than a sentence of death. In the earliest times "murder was punished by outlawry, but theft of goods and cattle by death." (Maitland.) The only hope that a condemned man might have is when a person came forward to take responsibility for him.

Notes for "On Democracy."

1. It was Edmund Burke (not Churchill as so many believe) who first said that "democracy is the only tolerable form into which human society can be thrown ..."

2. The British settlers, on coming to colonize the eastern seaboard of the North American continent, arrived with but a few physical possessions. What they did have, in full measure, was their love of freedom, a condition which very much defined them. The roots of democracy and freedom for all "western" democracies are planted in the rich history of Britain beginning with the *Magna Carta*. Enough to point out that when Captain Christopher Jones and his officers, together with their crew and their passengers disembarked from the *Mayflower*, in December of 1620, the pilgrims drew up a compact that provided for the government of the colony by the will of the majority.

3. In fact there is no specific date to which we can point. Human rights, a subject I deal with elsewhere, came about only through deep and long struggles culminating in historical declarations such as the *Magna Carta* (1215) and the *Petition of Right* (1628, "A man cannot be compelled to give evidence against himself"); but it is only with the *English Bill of Rights* of 1689 that we see any real progress in the evolution of law designed to protect the "rights" of the normal citizen. With the defeat of James at *The Battle of the Boyne*, the claim of divine right or hereditary right independent of law was formally brought to an end. Ever since, an English monarch is "as much the creature of an act of parliament as the pettiest tax-gatherer in his realm." (Green.)

4. We do not want our medical doctor doing what we want. Rather, in the final analysis, we want what the doctor thinks is best for our health and our life.

5. There is nothing new about this line of thinking, see John Stuart Mill. John Buchanan (The Nobel Laureate in Economic Science in 1986) and Gordon Tullock in their work, *The Calculus of Consent*, have shown in an "irrefutable way that whenever a minority is well organized and determined to bribe as many voters as necessary in order to have a majority ready to pass a desired decision, the majority rule works much more in favour of such minorities than is commonly supposed." (Leoni.)

6   In 1830 the British Commons represented an electorate of about 220,000 out of a total population of approximately 14 million, or about 3 percent of the adult population. (Leoni.)

7   It was Sir William Temple (1628-99), one of the architects of the *Glorious Revolution*, who was of the view that states often fell "under Tyrannies, which spring naturally out of Popular Governments." Since, this observation has proved to be true time and time again.

Notes for "Theory of Government."

1   This is known by those who study the subject as *The Paradox of Freedom*. There is nothing new about this; it was expressed by Plato. The argument as put by Karl Popper runs this way. "Freedom in the sense of absence of any restraining control must lead to very great restraint, since it makes the bully free to enslave the meek."

2   It took on hideous tones on account of the activities of the Russian terrorist Mikhail Bakunin (1814-76), his associates and imitators.

3   This is a false theory. See Popper's work, *The Poverty of Historicism*: "The fundamental thesis of this book [is that] the belief in historical destiny is sheer superstition, and that there can be no prediction of the course of human history by scientific or any other rational method ..."

4   If you understand the legal notion behind the legal words "common law" then you will understand that a great body of English law exists which was never written down, but still it was followed, and still it was enforced. The very strength of England, certainly in the past, is fully attributable to the stabilizing and enriching institution known as the common law.

5   The absence of fear brings peace, with peace people can lead productive lives; the group, together with its leader, will prosper. It is a valuable commodity, peace. The history books refer to it as the "Lord's Peace" or the "King's Peace."

6   Professor W. H. Hutt expressed it this way: "The term [individualism] is an extremely convenient one to express the views of those who would confine the functions of the State and various public authorities to a relatively small province, i.e.,

maintaining law and order, the army, the navy and other means of national defence, the enforcement of contracts, the maintenance of public services which cannot conveniently by entrusted to private enterprise, and in general the provision of a fair field for the play of individual energy." ("Individualism in Politics," as found Henry Hazlitt's book, *The Free Man's Library*.)

7   Henry George's (1839-97) fundamental remedy for poverty is a "single tax" levied on the value of land exclusive of improvements, and the abolition of all taxes which fall upon industry and thrift.

8   Ruskin likely had in mind the meaning of value rather than wealth.

9   Thus, we see about us devastation and ruin of all things which have no value as tradable property, whether it is breathable air or drinkable water, or the "goods and services" provided "free" by a socialistic government. It is on account of this principle, as is demonstrated in nature, that things gratuitously afforded by anybody, including the state, have little or no value. This, fundamentally, as attractive as the idea might be, is why socialism cannot work — people waste free stuff, always have and always will; it is in the nature of man to do so. We waste the free bounty of nature just as we waste the wealth of a country in a socialistic state.

10 Confucius lived during the turbulent times of the Chou dynasty (c.1027-256 BC). He urged a system of morality and statecraft to bring about peace, stability, and just government. Confucius was of the view that both the governed and those who govern were to be principled and virtuous; and that the first order of business for government was to instill in the population, as a whole, such virtues as to make good government easy. This was a system where one treated both inferiors and superiors with propriety. Confucianism laid down practical social concepts. Confucianism is not forced. It is not dogmatic. It is less a religion than it is an ethic by which people live.

11 See the writings of the French essayist, Montaigne (1533-1592).

12 "Power tends to corrupt and absolute power corrupts absolutely." This was contained in a letter written to Bishop Creighton in 1887.

13 "Masses are rude, lame, unmade, pernicious in their demands and influences, and need not to be flattered but to be schooled.

I wish not to concede anything to them, but to tame, drill, divide, and to break them up, and draw individuals out of them." (Ralph Waldo Emerson.)

14   We come to an understanding of what a natural law is by one, or by a combination of two ways. It is "implanted by nature in the human mind, or [is] capable of being demonstrated by reason." (*OED.*) The choice depends on one's philosophical view. Does a person come into this world with a blank mind, a *tabula rasa* and then, as life unfolds, acquires knowledge through the use of the five senses and a process of reflection. Or does a person come delivered and equipped with a primary set of ideas, innate ideas. The correct answer lies in either the ideas of Locke and the Empirical School, or Descartes and the Rational School.

15   One of the finest problems in legislation is to determine "what the state ought to take upon itself to direct by the public wisdom, and what it ought to leave, with as little interference as possible, to individual discretion." (Edmund Burke.)

16   Montesquieu was an admirer of John Locke, indeed, he spent two years (1729-31) in England. His work, *The Spirit of Laws*, written in 1748, held up the British Constitution to the admiration of the world. Montesquieu's doctrine on the separation of powers was picked up by the framers of the American constitution.

17   A great amount of the cost of past government, as measured in monetary terms, has ended up as government debt, which all of us carry. Government gross debt is in the billions and billions. The total is comprised of federal debt, provincial (state) and municipal debt. So too, there is the Canadian Pension Plan's unfunded liability. Most of this debt, because of the interest that must be paid periodically — over and over again — has seriously impacted on government expenditure in other areas, other areas which most of us might readily agree need government attention. And the bad times brought on by government spending (government spending always leads to inflation and/or taxation) impairs its credit with the international lenders to such an extent that it has no choice but to either tax more, or to inflate more, or to spend less; or any combination thereof. But if the government is not to exacerbate the problem, then it has no choice, at all — it must spend less and wait for things to self-correct.

18 Lest we forget, and as is amply demonstrated by history —
    Governments Kill. In the 20th century alone, it is estimated
    that governments have killed 170 million people. This is to be
    compared with the 133 million people who were murdered over
    the first several thousand years of human life, with China's
    emperors and the Mongols being classified as the top killers.
    It would seem that there is a correlation between the level of
    government power, to the level of those innocents who have
    been killed. But, Alas! This power/death relationship has not
    stopped people, wittingly, or not, from placing ever more and
    more power in the hands of those who control government which
    leads to ever more and more killing. This is easily demonstrated
    by a review of 20th century history. The most murderous system
    was the "Soviet Gulag State" — some 62 million died, most
    through communistic state policy of committing genocide:
    the Don Cossacks, Ukrainian peasants, and Estonians. The
    communists even resorted to killing themselves as massive
    purges were carried out by the communist party. The communist
    regime in Russia, over a 75 year period, killed 35 million men,
    women and children — all in the interests of state planning. The
    communists of 20th century China, too, have carried on with
    China's sad and ancient record of mass murder. Hitler, with
    his ovens, ranks 3rd in the 20th century for mass murder. He
    and his henchmen of the Third Reich killed 21 million of those
    whom they felt did not fit in with their vision of things. The
    state planners in Russia, China and Germany, as we can see,
    for the 20th century, take the top three prizes. On this dismal
    and deadly list of 20th century governments who butcher their
    people, we will also see: Japan, Cambodia, Vietnam, North
    Korea, Turkey, Poland, Rumania, Yugoslavia, and Mexico. All
    have killed their dissenters and in the process have received
    little attention from the rest of us. (We will not include in the
    analysis, the terror bombings of civilian populations during the
    Second World War by Great Britain and the U.S. whereby 816,000
    innocent people died.) These are the grim, government, killing
    figures from both our long and recent past. But let me remind
    you, government killing continues, to-day: in Afghanistan, in
    Angola, in Bosnia, in Chechnya, in Georgia, in Iraq, in Liberia,

and in Rwanda, and in country, after country, after country. (The figures set out in this note are taken from Rummel's work.)

Notes for "Politics and The Lie of Legitimacy."

1   Lippmann, in a footnote to this passage, quoted James Trunslow Adams, as follows: "As we look over the list of the early leaders of the republic, Washington, John Adams, Hamilton, and others, we discern that they were all men who insisted upon being themselves and who refused to truckle to the people. With each succeeding generation, the growing demand of the people that its elective officials shall not lead but merely register the popular will has steadily undermined the independence of those who derive their power from popular election. The persistent refusal of the Adamses to sacrifice the integrity of their own intellectual and moral standards and values for the sake of winning public office or popular favour is another of the measuring rods by which we may measure the divergence of American life from its starting point."

2   A leader is one who is possessed of the supreme gift of gathering up and expressing the ideas which thousands of others feel but cannot express. There is no message so effective as to tell people what they know already, to hold a mirror to their face and a sound board to their voice.

3   The greatest compensation to one who has achieved an elected office is the value to him as the incumbent to be able to use his office so to get himself elected once again. A strong "elected" leader will ride herd over his staff; it is through staff that he exercises power and often, at least he believes, that it is through staff he maintains power straight on through to the next election. Any vast and highly organized social institution — whether it is an army, or a union, or a large commercial company, or a government — becomes taken over by the "wire-pullers" the "bosses" and the "permanent officials."

4   The leaders are not the choice of the people as much as they are the choice of the political wirepullers. In the United States (forgetting for the moment how they got on the ballet), the leadership candidates are at least on the ballet. Not so in Canada, the Canadian people have no direct say as to who the leader is to be, and, seem to give the matter not an once of concern.

5   "To procure unanimity, to get men to act in *corps*, we must
    appeal for the most part to gross and obvious motives, to
    authority and passion, to their vices, not their virtues: we must
    discard plain truth and abstract justice as doubtful and efficient
    pleas, retaining only the names and the pretext as a convenient
    salvo for hypocrisy." (William Hazlitt.) "[Politicians] hold their
    offices for a short time, and to do this they must maneuver and
    manipulate combinations ... stuff of daily life in a democracy ...
    in the daily routine of democratic politics, elected executives
    can never for long take their eyes from the mirror of the
    constituencies. They must not look too much out of the window
    at the realities beyond." (Lippmann.)

6   "The competitive odds are heavily against the candidate who,
    like Burke with the electors of Bristol, promises to be true to
    his own best reason and judgment. The odds are all in favor of
    the candidate who offers himself as the agent, the delegate, the
    spokesman, the errand boy, of blocs of voters." (Lippmann.)

7   Assuming that the typical voter has the intellect and can take
    the time away from making a living so to study any particular
    issue and come to a stand on it, the exercise is a crap shoot.
    "All voting is a sort of gaming, like checkers or backgammon,
    with a slight moral tinge to it, a playing with right and wrong,
    with moral questions; and betting naturally accompanies it. The
    character of the voters is not staked. I cast my vote, perchance,
    as I think right; but I am not vitally concerned that right should
    prevail. I am willing to leave it to the majority. Its obligation,
    therefore, never exceeds that of expediency. Even voting for the
    right is doing nothing for it. It is only expressing to men feebly
    your desire that it should prevail. A wise man will not leave the
    right to the mercy of chance, nor wish it to prevail through the
    power of the majority. There is but little virtue in the action of
    masses of men." [Henry David Thoreau (1817-62).]

8   For example, is it to be supposed that the average voter
    understands the fundamental principles of economics? That
    he does not is excusable. Is it to be supposed that the average
    politician understands the fundamental principles of economics?
    That he does not is inexcusable. Sir James Fitzjames Stephen:
    "... there are and always will be in the world an enormous mass
    of bad or indifferent people — people who deliberately do all

sorts of things which they ought not to do, and leave undone all sorts of things which they ought to do. Estimate the proportion of men and women who are selfish, frivolous, idle, absolutely commonplace and wrapped up in the smallest of petty routines, and consider how far the freest of free discussion is likely to improve them. The only way by which it is practically possible to act upon them at all is by compulsion or restraint."

9   In corporate law there is the notion of a "special resolution" where important decisions can only be taken where 75% vote in its favor.

10   "The temper of George the First was that of a gentleman usher; and his one care was to get money for his favorites and himself. The temper of George the Second was that of a drill-sergeant, who believed himself master of his realm." (Green.) As parliament by this age was all powerful, it could nonetheless be bought by "places, pensions, and other bribes" — sound familiar?

11   Arthur James Balfour (1848-1930), Britain's Prime Minister through the years 1902-06. These quotes of Balfour's were taken from his introduction to Bagehot's *The English Constitution*.

12   "... much argument is not required to guide the public, still less a formal exposition of that argument. What is mostly needed is the manly utterance of clear conclusions; if a statesman gives these in a felicitous way (and if with a few light and humorous illustrations, so much the better), he has done his part." (Bagehot, *The English Constitution*.)

13   Authority intoxicates,
And makes mere sots of magistrates;
The fumes of it invade the brain,
And make men giddy, proud, and vain ...:
By this the fool commands the wise,
The noble with the base complies,
The sot assumes the rule of wit,
And cowards make the brave submit.
        — Butler's *Hudibras*, 1680.

Notes for "The Siren's Song."

1   Socialism is "a theory or policy of social organization which aims at or advocates the ownership and control of the means of production, capital, land, property, etc., by the community as a

whole, and their administration or distribution in the interests of all." (*OED*.) Or more simply, a state of society in which things are held or used in common. Collectivism, socialism, communism: it's all the same. A communist, incidentally, it has been said, is merely a socialist with the courage to express his views openly and with conviction. And, the theory of communism may be summed up in the single sentence: "Abolition of private property." (Marx, 1848.) Therefore we see essentially that socialism is, as H. G. Wells put it, "a repudiation of the idea of ownership in the light of the public good." The question essentially boils down to property rights, a subject on which I have written.

2   Joseph A. Schumpeter, an economist whom the socialists love to claim as their own, stated the principal difficulty: "Any kind of centralist socialism, therefore, can successfully clear the first hurdle — logical definiteness and consistency of socialist planning — and we may as well negotiate the next one at once. It consists of the 'practical impossibility' on which, it seems, most anti-socialist economists are at present inclined to retire after having accepted defeat on the purely logical issue. They hold that our central board would be confronted with a task of unmanageable complication, and some of them add that in order to function the socialist arrangement would presuppose a wholesale reformation of souls or of behavior — whichever way we prefer to style it — which historical experience and common sense prove to be out of the question."

3   "A cardinal trait in all advancing organizations is the development of the regulative apparatus. If the parts of a whole are to act together, there must be appliances by which their actions are directed; and in proportion as the whole is large and complex, and has many requirements to be met by many agencies, the directive apparatus must be extensive, elaborate, and powerful. That it is thus with individual organisms needs no saying; and that it must be thus with social organisms is obvious." (Seldon.)

4   It was James Anthony Froude (1818-94) who said: "The first principle, on which the theory of a science of history can be plausibly argued, is that all actions whatsoever arise from self-interest. It may be enlightened self-interest, it may be unenlightened; but it is assumed as an axiom, that every man, in

whatever he does, is aiming at something which he considered will promote his happiness. His conduct is not determined by his will; it is determined by the object of his desire. Adam Smith, in laying the foundations of political economy, expressly eliminates every other motive. He does not say that men never act on other motives; still less, that they never ought to act on other motives. He asserts merely that, as far as the arts of production are concerned, and of buying and selling, the action of self-interest may be counted upon as uniform." Then there is Ralph Waldo Emerson: "On the whole, selfishness plants best, prunes best, makes the best commerce and the best citizen." ("Montaigne," *Representative Men*.) And finally, if one is truly proceeding in what is in his best interest, he will be kind and considerate to all those around him; a rational person will not normally do things for momentary gain if he thinks the action will cause him grief in the future. "Caution," as Woodrow Wilson said, "is the confidential agent of selfishness."

5   See the philosophy of Sir Karl Popper and in particular *The Open Society and Its Enemies* (1945). The guiding public policy put forward by Popper in this grand work of his, is this: "Minimize avoidable suffering," this in contradistinction to the Utilitarian view, "Maximize happiness."

6   John Stuart Mill (1806-1873) was an English philosopher and economist. Though socialists will often misquote him and claim him for their own — they cannot, for John Stuart Mill was, pure and simple, a believer in the necessity, for the benefit of the whole, of the freedom of choice for the individual, and stressed in his writings the danger of putting too much power in the hands of the state.

7   Popper was of the view that any "social engineer" can only proceed on a "piecemeal" basis. "... only a minority of social institutions are consciously designed while the vast majority have just 'grown' as the results of human actions." (See *The Poverty of Historicism*.) I would venture to give but a couple of examples of the consciously designed social institutions: the government mechanisms themselves (legislative, executive and judicial), national armed forces (fully answerable to the proper political authorities), local police forces, jails, food inspection, health inspection and school inspection. Certain social institutions would arise quite naturally as the result of human interaction:

there is the all important activity of food production and distribution, housing and clothing — all of which have arisen and maintain themselves quite nicely, thank-you, without government intervention. I would also include the delivery of health care and education, notwithstanding that there are those (invariably on the government payroll) who would be aghast to think that these (admittedly) important social institutions should be left to the free market to sort out, hoping, as they do, that the taxpayer will forget that fortunes are being spent by government with, demonstratively, poor results.

8   That the political process is treated with disdain or wholly ignored by millions, is evident by the turn out at election time. Compare this with the market system where all the voters spend every dollar with infinitely more thought, knowledge and responsibility.

9   *The Law Society Gazette*, vol. 28, p. 201.

10 Robert Owen (1771-1858) was the man that came up with the word socialism. Born in Wales, Owen became apprenticed to a linen draper, but through "pluck and luck" soon found himself a part owner in a large spinning establishment in Manchester. In time he bought himself a set of mills in the squalid village of New Lanark. He then set out to "govern men by reason" and to "overturn bigotry and superstition."

11 The scientific method might be best summed up by stating that all conclusions in science are empirical, tentative, and undogmatic. Scientific theory has its roots in the Humeian view that all concepts must be built with ideas of substance, ideas of matter which truly exist in the external world and not figments of pure imagination — ideas consistent with all observed phenomena. The approach calls for the gathering in of all observations, all the available pieces of the puzzle, so to speak; and, then, to use the imagination to fill in the gaps, sufficient to make a statement about the whole, a supposition, a theory. We then (at least we ought to) proceed to conduct our affairs on the basis of this theory, until we come onto a piece of evidence that doesn't fit the theory. It is at this point we ought to adjust the theory, not only to fit the new observation but the old observations too. And then to set out once again.

12 "The rich have become richer, and the poor have become poorer; and the vessel of state is driven between Scylla and Charybdis

of anarchy and despotism." Shelley, the romanticist, in his *Defence of Poetry* speaks of another time, a time when the landed gentry owned it all, and democracy had yet come to full bloom. Shelley's quote, though, has as much application today as it ever did. Instead of the royal aristocrats versus the have-not people, we have today those who are at the government tax taps and those who are taxed. The sliver of the whole — the poor and disadvantaged — hardly count when it comes to the larger discussion.

13   I editorialize and say that there is no need to pass a law where there exists a moral duty. This is simply because moral actions occur to a greater degree and to a greater extent than any law compelling the same action. Moral actions automatically come about without the expense and rancor of passing and enforcing law.

14   There is an agenda being served in Canada in our fight against poverty, and I fear it is not the agenda of the poor. We might define poverty at least in two ways. The first way is to establish "official poverty lines," this is how Statistics Canada has defined it. This is a relative definition of poverty, it focuses on a person's standard of living in comparison to others within the community. This approach presumes that we as human beings measure our well being in relation to what others enjoy. By this definition we are poor if our standard of living is substantially below what most others have, regardless of whether we have met our basic needs or not. This concept of our basic needs brings us to the second definition. One is poor where he or she cannot acquire all the basic needs for physical survival. This is the more traditional way of defining poverty. It is an absolute and not a relative definition. To accept the first definition means that most all of us are poor, as most everybody will find someone else who possesses more stuff. While under the second definition a state of poverty will only exist if there exists a situation of genuine deprivation of certain of the necessities of life, a situation in which the physical well being of a person is threatened, a situation where the person is on the borders of being cold, hungry and sick. To accept the relative definition of income is to accept there are, where every one is equally deprived, no poor people in Somalia. To accept that in an economic depression, given that every one's income decreases

is to accept that there are no more poor in the country than there was before the depression began. Thus we see why socialists readily adopt the relative definition of poverty. To adopt such a definition means one must accept the manner in which poverty is to be fought, viz. to redistribute income and property from those who have more to those who have less. It may well be a worthwhile object to redistribute wealth, but it is not honest and brings fog to the field of battle when we redistribute wealth in the name of fighting poverty.

15 In Plato's scheme, families, at least in the upper classes, were to be abolished, children were to be raised collectively, women, well, they were to be shared! "... women shall be common to all men, and none shall cohabit with any privately, and that the children shall be common, and that no parent shall know its own offspring nor any child its parent."

16 Seldon. "... since the power to persuade and organize others in collective organizations is itself unequal, the ability of people to advance as individuals in the market without waiting for others is in the end more egalitarian than the socialist method of waiting in the political process for agreement, universal or by majorities, in debating chambers. The evolutionary spontaneous freedom under capitalism for individuals to act without collective restraint is necessary for some to forge ahead and show the others the way. In the end, as the others follow, more can share in the advance. Inequality in action is the way to equality in result."

17 "The great principle, that societies and laws exist only for the purpose of increasing the sum of private happiness, is not recognized with sufficient clearness. The good of the body, distinct from the good of the members, and sometimes hardly compatible with the good of the members, seems to be the object which he proposes himself. Of all political fallacies, this has perhaps had the widest and the most mischievous operation." (Macaulay's, "Machiavelli.")

18 The chief problem with social "scientists" is that they confuse, as Sir Karl Popper pointed out, laws with trends.

19 Popper likens "social science" to "midwifery." It is the mother who is obliged to go through the untidy and the painful business of delivering her baby. An important point that is to be made, by the way, is that not only can a state not be run by a controlling

mind, but it cannot, as the Roman statesman, Cicero, pointed out, be set by one controlling mind. A lasting state can only evolve through the passing of several generations. It comes into being only after the passage of a considerable period of time. "Our state, on the contrary, is not due to the personal creation of one man, but of very many; it has not been founded during the lifetime of any particular individual, but through a series of centuries and generations. For he said that there never was in the world a man so clever as to foresee everything and that even if we could concentrate all brains into the head of one man, it would be impossible for him to provide for everything at one time without having the experience that comes from practice through a long period of history." (As quoted by Leoni.)

_____

REFERENCES

(Note: see www.blupete.com for specific page references.)

Acton, *Collected Works and Essays of Lord Acton*, Fears, ed. (Indianapolis: Liberty Classics, 1985).

Arguments and Speeches by Eminent Lawyers, A Collection of ... (New York: Baker, Voorhis & Co., 1882).

Bagehot, *The English Constitution*, 1867 (Oxford University Press, 1928).

—, *Biographical Studies* (London: Longmans, Green; 1889).

Bastiat, *The Law*, 1850.

Benet's, Reader's Encyclopedia (Harper & Row, 1987).

Bentham, *The Principles of Morals and Legislation*, 1780.

—, *The Principles of the Civil Code*.

Blackstone, *Commentaries*, 1765-9.

Buchanan and Tullock, *The Calculus of Consent*, 1962.

Burke, *The Works ...* (Oxford University Press, 6 vols., nd).

Canadian Criminal Code of 1892, The Genesis of the ... (The Osgoode Society, University of Toronto Press, 1989).

Cardozo, *Law and Literature*, 1931.

Carlyle, *Heroes*, 1858.

Chambers Biographical Dictionary (Edinburgh) (*Chambers*).

Church, *Voyage Home*, 1964.

Durant, *The Story of Civilization* (New York: Simon & Schuster, 1954-75).

—, *The Lessons of History* (New York: Simon & Schuster, 1968).

Emerson, *Representative Men*, 1860.

—, *Essays* (New York: Nelson, nd).

Federalists Papers, The, 1787-8.

George, *Progress and Poverty*, 1879.

Gest, *The Lawyers in Literature* (Boston: The Boston Book Co., 1913).

Green, *History of the English People*, 1877-80.

Hayek, *The Fatal Conceit, The Errors of Socialism* (University of Chicago Press, Vol. I, 1989).

Hazlitt (Henry), *The Free Man's Library* (Princeton, N.J., Van Nostrand, 1956).

Hazlitt (William), *Table-Talk*, 1822.

—, *The Spirit of the Age*, 1825.

http://www.blupete.com/Literature/Essays/TableHazIII.htm

Hazlitt (William),, *The Plain Speaker*, 1826.

Hobbes, *Leviathan*, 1660.

Hume, *An Enquiry Concerning Human Understanding*, 1748.

—, Political Discourses, 1752.

Huxley (Aldous), *Themes & Variations* (New York: Harper, 1st Ed., 1950).

Jefferson, *Notes on Virginia*, 1782.

Kirk, *Edmund Burke: A Genius Reconsidered* (Arlington House, 1967).

Leacock, *Our Heritage of Liberty* (London: Bodley Head, 1942).

Leoni, *Freedom and the Law* (Indianapolis: Liberty Press, 3rd Ed., 1991).

Lippmann, *The Public Philosophy* (Boston: Little, Brown; 1955).

Locke, *Two Treatises of Government*, 1690.

—, *Essay Concerning Human Understanding*, 1690.

Macaulay, *Critical, Historical and Miscellaneous Essays* (New York: Sheldon, 6 vols., 1862).

Maitland, *History of English Law*, 1895.

Malthus, *Definitions in Political Economy*, 1827.

Mill, *Principles of Political Economy*, 1848.

—, On Liberty, 1859.

—, *Consideration on Representative Government*, 1861.

Montesquieu, *The Spirit of Laws*, 1748.

Oxford English Dictionary (*OED*).

Phillips, *Shakespeare and the Lawyers* (London: Methuen & CO., 1972).

Popper, *The Open Society and Its Enemies*, 1945.

—, *The Poverty of Historicism*, 1957.

—, *Popper Selections*, David Miller, ed. (Princeton University Press, 1985).

Priestley, *Lectures in History*, 1788.

Radzinowicz, *History of Criminal Law and Its Administration* (London: Stevens & Sons Limited, 1948).

Rasmussen and Benson, *The Economic Anatomy of a Drug War*.

Rummel, *Death by Government* (Transaction Publishers, 1997).

Ruskin, *Ethics of the Dust*, 1865.

Saleilles, *The Individualization of Punishment* (Boston: Little, Brown & Co., 1911).

Schumpeter, *Capitalism, Socialism and Democracy* (1942) (Harper & Row, 3rd ed., 1962).

Seldon, *Capitalism* (Oxford: Blackwell, 1991).

Spencer, *First Principles* (London: Williams & Norgate, 1875).

—, *A Plea for Liberty, An Argument Against Socialism and Socialistic Legislation*, 1891.

Spooner *Reader, A Lysander* ... (San Francisco: Fox & Wilkes, 1992).

Stephen, *Liberty, Equality, Fraternity*, 1873.

—, *History of the Criminal Law*, 1883.

Stevenson, *Seven Theories of Human Nature* (Oxford University Press, 1987).

Sumner, *The Family and Property*, 1888.

Tolstoy, *The Slavery of our Times*, 1900.

Traill, *Social England*, 1893-97.

Trevelyan (George Macaulay), *England Under Queen Anne: 1702-1714* (London: Longmans, Green; 1948).

—, *An Autobiography & Other Essays* (London: Longmans, Green; July, 1949).

Von Ruville, *William Pitt, Earl of Chatham* (London: Heinemann, 1907).

Wade, *Administrative Law* (Oxford University Press, 6th ed., 1988).

White, *Famous Utopias of the Renaissance* (Chicago: Packard, 1946).

———————